Law for Doctors:
Principles and Practicalities

Third edition

Law for Doctors:
Principles and Practicalities
Third edition

John Paul Garside LLB LLM

Solicitor of the Supreme Court of England and Wales

Head of Legal Services
Norfolk and Norwich University Hospital

Foreword by
Margaret Branthwaite MD FRCP FFARCS

Barrister, Lincoln's Inn

Formerly Consultant Physician and Anaesthetist
Royal Brompton Hospital, London

The ROYAL
SOCIETY *of*
MEDICINE
PRESS *Limited*

First edition (2000)   by MA Branthwaite
Second edition (2002)   by MA Branthwaite and
                          NW Beresford MB ChB LLB Barrister, Lincoln's Inn

© 2006 Royal Society of Medicine Press Ltd

Published by the Royal Society of Medicine Press Ltd
1 Wimpole Street, London W1G 0AE, UK
Tel: +44 (0)20 7290 2921
Fax: +44 (0)20 7290 2929
E-mail: publishing@rsm.ac.uk
Website: www.rsmpress.co.uk

British Library Cataloguing in Publication Data
A catalogue record for this book is available from the British Library

ISBN 1-85315-681-7

Distribution in Europe and Rest of World
Marston Book Services Ltd
PO Box 269, Abingdon
Oxon OX14 4YN, UK
Tel: +44 (0)1235 465500
Fax: +44 (0)1235 465555
E-mail: direct.order@marston.co.uk

Distribution in the USA and Canada
Royal Society of Medicine Press Ltd
c/o BookMasters Inc., 30 Amberwood Parkway
Ashland, OH 44805, USA
Tel: +1 800 247 6553/+1 800 266 5564
Fax: +1 419 281 6883
E-mail: order@bookmasters.com

Distribution in Australia and New Zealand
Elsevier Australia
30–52 Smidmore Street
Marrikville, NSW 2204, Australia
Tel: +61 2 9517 8999
Fax: +61 2 9517 2249
E-mail: service@elsevier.com.au

Editorial services and typesetting by GM & BA Haddock, Ford, Midlothian, UK
Printed in the UK by Bell & Bain Ltd, Glasgow

Contents

1. Structure and sources of English law   1

Similarities between medicine and the law – differences between medicine
and the law (the role of caselaw) – legal precedent and the common law – the
role of policy considerations in judicial decision-making – statutory law –
European law – the civil and criminal justice system – the purposes of the law –
the law in Scotland, Northern Ireland and other jurisdictions – legislative basis
for the regulation of healthcare – sources of legal information

2. Principles of negligence, duty and standard of care   11

Legal basis for claims arising from clinical practice – duty of care –
standard of care – inexperienced staff – vicarious liability

3. Foreseeability and causation   19

The burden and standard of proof – foreseeability – injury – causation of injury
– injury caused by failure to act – *res ipsa loquitur* 'the thing speaks for itself'

4. Financial considerations: compensation and costs   25

General damages – special damages – future losses (the concept of
multiplier and multiplicand) – structured settlements/periodic payments –
provisional damages – some specific elements of loss – possible future
developments – funding litigation – Legal Aid – Conditional Fee
Agreements – funding the defence of clinical negligence claims

5. Legal procedure; dispute resolution; role of expert witnesses   33

Parties to the action – limitation – clinical negligence pre-action protocol –
disclosure of medical records – Letter of Claim – response to the Letter of
Claim – resolution without legal proceedings – legal proceedings – defending

a claim – subsequent conduct – without prejudice correspondence – alternative dispute resolution (ADR) – role of the expert witness

6. Confidentiality and disclosure 41

Relevant statutory provisions – disclosure of medical records – disclosure in the context of litigation – breach of confidentiality in the public interest – legal professional privilege – disclosure of medical records after death – is there a duty of *post-facto* candour?

7. Consent; minors and the mentally incapacitated; research; training 49

The nature of consent – what constitutes valid consent? – was consent given voluntarily? – what constitutes 'sufficient information'? – assessing mental competence and the refusal of consent to treatment – treatment without consent – parental responsibility and consent by or on behalf of children and young people – consent on behalf of the mentally incompetent/incapacitated adult – consent for research and teaching

8. Complaints, whistle-blowing and disciplinary proceedings 61

NHS complaints procedure – the NHS complaints system in practice – private sector complaints – whistle-blowing – professional regulatory proceedings – further regulatory control – action by employing authorities

9. Doctors and the coroner's court 71

Duty to inform the coroner – the coroner's post mortem examination – retention of post mortem tissue – coroners and the *Human Rights Act* – pre-inquest reviews – the inquest – the coroner's jury – the coroner's verdict – recommendations by the coroner – challenge to decisions of the coroner – review and reform of death certification and investigation

10. Doctors and the criminal law 81

Assault – homicide – manslaughter by gross negligence – criminal liability for end-of-life decisions ('mercy killing' and withdrawal of treatment) – withholding or withdrawing life-sustaining treatment – the law as a vehicle for social change

Glossary 91

Index 93

Foreword

Medical law is the interface between two long-established and, some would say, reactionary professions. But although practitioners within each discipline have always had need of at least some knowledge of the other, the differences in terminology, objectives, practice and manner of presentation have often created barriers to good communication and reciprocal understanding between clinicians and lawyers. Until recently, it is the law which has had most need for recourse to specialist medical evidence for the just resolution of claims, prosecutions or inquiries involving personal injury or death. But lawyers can frame their questions with greater accuracy and seek advice from more appropriate specialists if they already have some understanding of medicine and, to serve this objective, the Royal Society of Medicine began during the closing years of the twentieth century to offer a programme of lectures entitled 'Medicine for Lawyers'. Prompted by the obvious benefit of offering such insight into the principles and practice of medicine and conscious of the ever-increasing intrusion of law into the day-to-day practice of medicine, I suggested there be a corresponding course 'Law for Doctors'. The first was held in the spring of 2000 and a set of lecture notes was envisaged to accompany it. But, apart from specialist legal textbooks, little published material on the law as it related to clinicians was available at the time and so it seemed worthwhile to expand the anticipated lecture notes into a small handbook, intended to be 'user-friendly' to clinicians and other health care professionals. The Royal Society of Medicine Press undertook production, and publication of the First edition coincided with the first lecture programme. Since then, copies of the book have formed the course material for succeeding lecture programmes and this tradition is being maintained with the publication of this, the third edition.

But change is inevitable. As the original author, I was mindful of the benefit I had derived from training and experience in both medicine and the law, describing it facetiously as being able to run with the hare and hunt with the hounds. But it was more than a personal benefit – a background in clinical practice helped, in some subtle way, to make the sometimes harsh lessons of the law less irksome to audiences involved in the day-to-day practice of medicine. To me, therefore, it was imperative that those who subsequently assumed responsibility for both the book and the lecture series should themselves have a background in both disciplines. So I was delighted to work with Dr Nigel Beresford on the Second edition and now I am equally delighted to welcome John Paul Garside who has undertaken a comprehensive revision for this third edition. In the introductory pages, he modestly conceals the diversity of his background, but experience within the intensive care unit at Great Ormond Street Hospital preceded his qualification as a barrister and work in private practice before he re-entered the health service and transferred to the role of solicitor.

It is now four years since the Second edition of *Law for Doctors* and much has happened within that interval to change the medicolegal interface. Pressure from the public, the media, from within both professions and from governmental sources have all increased the intensity of legal scrutiny and control over the practice of medicine. It is all the more essential, therefore, that clinicians have some knowledge not only of how to apply relevant law but also how the law can impinge on their own daily practice. In seeking to fulfil this requirement, the objectives of *Law for Doctors* have not changed since the First edition but the content most certainly has. I am indebted to John Paul Garside for assuming responsibility for bringing the book up to date and am conscious that he has discharged this remit handsomely despite many other pressures. I am delighted to see *Law for Doctors* continue under this entirely new authorship and trust it will secure the success it deserves.

M. Branthwaite
London, May 2006

Preface

A profession's most valuable asset is its collective reputation and the confidence which that inspires.
Sir Thomas Bingham MR (*Bolton v Law Society [1994] 1 WLR 512*)

The reputation of the medical profession has suffered some significant blows in the years since the First edition of this book. In the aftermath of a series of well-publicised scandals, including those that prompted the Bristol heart-surgery inquiry, the Shipman inquiry and the nation-wide response to the retention of organs at Alder Hey Hospital, the automatic presumption of beneficence – that doctors will always act in their patients' best interests – has been cast into doubt. The courts now adopt a less deferential approach to the medical profession than has historically been the case and there is an increased awareness of individual patient rights. This is of particular significance because the incorporation into English Law of the European Convention of Human Rights has given rise to new lines of argument with respect to issues that were previously thought to be settled. More generally, our healthcare systems are subject to ever closer scrutiny, both by the media and regulators. It has, therefore, never been more important for doctors, and medical students who wish to follow in their footsteps, to be acquainted with the legal context to clinical practice.

The law is a strange entity, a mixture of principle, pragmatism, wisdom and historical anachronism. It is sometimes likened to a maze, through which a lawyer must guide his client. My hope is that this book will continue to offer, as it has in previous editions, an insight into the law as it operates in relation to medicine. I have endeavoured to remain true to the concept of the book as an overview of the subject in no more than 100 pages. More detail is included in areas of controversy or particular judicial, legislative or regulatory activity, especially in relation to consent (Chapter 7) and coroners (Chapter 9). Throughout the text, signposts are given to additional information that may not be readily accessible elsewhere for those who, for whatever reason, have cause for particular interest. The number of case 'vignettes' and references has also been increased and updated in response to positive comments on earlier editions.

I offer my particular thanks to Vikki Rant, Alison Brockhurst and Frances Dyson for their assistance in the preparation of this book.

Needless to say, the contents of this book are intended for purposes of general guidance and specific advice should be sought in individual cases from legal advisors, trustworthy colleagues or a clinical ethics committee. To the best of my knowledge, the law is stated correctly as of 31 March 2006 although in some cases later additions have been possible.

JP Garside
Norwich, April 2006

Preface to Second edition

Changes in legal procedure introduced in response to Lord Woolf's report into civil justice are now well integrated into practice and so require less emphasis in an introductory text. Some chapters in this new edition have, therefore, been condensed or eliminated. New material has been introduced to amplify the section on confidentiality and the disclosure of records, and the text has otherwise been updated to incorporate new statute and caselaw since April 2000. To the best of our knowledge, the law is stated correctly as at 1 October 2002.

MA Branthwaite and NW Beresford
London, November 2002

Preface to First edition

Few sources of medical law are easily accessible to medical practitioners, and research is hindered by unfamiliar legal terminology and style. And yet the law is impinging on medical practice ever more frequently and creates anxiety which is exacerbated by the impotence of ignorance. 'Legal paternalism' is accepted, often gratefully, but is no more appropriate today than its medical equivalent in patient care. This book sets out to provide health care professionals, particularly doctors, with sufficient understanding of the law to alleviate as far as possible those elements of concern which are founded on uncertainty, to assist them to participate more fully in discussions and decisions on cases with which they are involved and, above all, to have some idea of what to expect, be they required to assist the court or face legal action themselves. The content is restricted to those aspects of the law which involve medical practitioners most often.

The style of a medical rather than a legal textbook has been adopted. Case reports (legal authorities) are identified numerically and collected together at the end of each chapter as references. They are also listed alphabetically in a Table of Cases at the beginning of the book, preceded by a key to the accepted abbreviations for relevant series. Wherever possible, the citation in *Medical Law Reports* has been chosen in preference to other legal sources. This series began in 1989 and is available at the library of The Royal Society of Medicine, as is a textbook of medical caselaw incorporating synopses of the most important actions reported before 1990. Statutes referred to in the text are listed after the Table of Cases. There is a glossary of legal terms before the index, and more detailed sources of medical law are identified at the end of Chapter one. In accordance with section 6 of the *Interpretation Act 1978*, masculine pronouns are used throughout to indicate persons of either gender.

To the best of my knowledge and belief, the law is stated correctly as at 1 April 2000.

MA Branthwaite
London, April 2000

Law Reports – Abbreviations

Where possible, use is made in this text of the neutral case citations, which have been available since 2001. Most cases cited in this way may be accessed free of charge through the internet sources identified in Chapter 1. Such citations denote jurisdiction and court and the date of judgement.

Thus, for example:

➤ *Rees v Darlington Memorial Hospital NHS Trust [2003] UKHL 52* was heard in the UK House of Lords in 2003; whereas

➤ *Lillywhite & Anor v University College London Hospitals NHS Trust [2005] EWCA Civ 1466* was heard in the Court of Appeal (England and Wales) Civil Division; and

➤ *An NHS Trust v MB [2006] EWHC 507 (Fam)* was heard in the High Court Family Division.

In other, typically older, cases use is made of the traditional Law Reports series, identified by accepted abbreviations as below:

AC	Appeal Cases (Decisions of the House of Lords)
All ER	All England Reports
BMLR	Butterworths Medical Law Reports
Crim LR	Criminal Law Reports
ECHR	European Court of Human Rights
FLR	Family Law Reports
JP	Justice of the Peace Reports
Lloyd's Rep Med	Lloyd's Law Reports: Medical (continuation since 1998 of Medical Law Reports)
Med LR	Medical Law Reports
MLC	Medical Law Cases
QBD (or KBD)	Queen's (or King's) Bench Division (of High Court)
WLR	Weekly Law Reports

SOME EXAMPLES

Civil case citation

Bolam v Frien Hospital Management Committee [1957] 1 WLR 583 – referred to in speech as 'Bolam and/versus Frien Hospital Management Committee' or

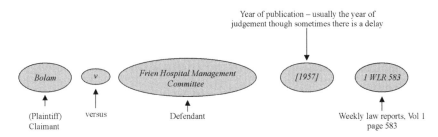

'Bolam':

Criminal case citation

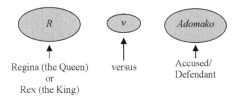

R v Adomako [1994] 5 Med LR 277 – referred to in speech as 'the Crown and Adomako' or 'Adomako':

Judicial Review cases

R (on the application of Rogers) v Swindon NHS PCT & Secretary of State for Health [2006] EWCA Civ 392

Application for court declaration

Such cases are heard in the Family Division and the identity of the Parties is anonymised. Some detail may, however, be provided to assist in determining the subject matter of the case.

Re AK (Medical Treatment :Consent) [2001] 1 FLR 129

Re A (Minors) (Conjoined Twins: Separation) [2000] EWCA Civ 254

Table of cases

Entries identify the chapter and the numbered reference within it.

Table of Statutes

The reference is to the page on which each Act is mentioned.

Structure and sources of
English law

Similarities between medicine and the law

Medicine and the law share a number of common characteristics. The practical applications of medicine divide broadly into medicine (physic) and surgery, the law into civil and criminal practice. Practitioners of either discipline require prolonged training, with academic (preclinical) studies preceding vocational (clinical) training, followed by a period of quasi-apprenticeship (pupil/trainee or house officer). Specialisation is common after full registration (call to the Bar/admission to the Roll) and practitioners may choose to adopt a continuing professional relationship with clients (GP or solicitor), or a consultative role sought only in particular circumstances (specialist or counsel).

Medicine and surgery both divide into sub-specialities and so too do civil and criminal law. Tort, or interpersonal wrong-doing short of criminality, is a sub-division of civil law, which includes 'wrongs' such as negligence, nuisance, defamation and trespass to the person. Another sub-division, the law of contract, deals with disputes arising from legally enforceable agreements, although contracts for the sale of land are considered separately again. The boundaries of these legal sub-divisions are not always clear cut, any more than they are in medicine.

Most litigation against medical practitioners consists of claims for the tort of negligence, although private practice also spawns claims for breach of contract. As in medicine, there is some overlap even between the primary sub-divisions; for example, gastrointestinal haemorrhage can be managed medically or surgically. Similarly, assault and battery can constitute either a criminal offence, or the civil wrong (tort) of trespass to the person. In exceptional cases, negligence is deemed so gross as to warrant prosecution as a criminal offence.

Differences between medicine and the law – the role of caselaw

The similarities set out above are matched by significant differences, the most important being sources of knowledge and the way in which these are applied. Modern medicine is founded on scientific study, which may provoke changes to the recommended approach to particular illnesses or conditions. Medical case reports are little more than interesting curiosities, providing examples of a particular condition or treatment; they do not bind future practice.

By contrast, English common law is built upon caselaw – the body of decided judgements in individual cases, through which legal principles have been established or 'found'. These principles are then applied in subsequent cases unless the new matter can be distinguished on its facts from all the preceding decisions, or a new and cogent argument for change can be advanced. A single case report, sometimes of considerable antiquity, can suffice to resolve a contested point unless that decision has been specifically over-ruled by a more recent judgement from a higher court.

Legal precedent and the common law

The term 'precedent' describes the binding power of previous decisions on subsequent, similar cases. It is intended to secure parity of treatment and consistency of approach. Decisions in the High Court are binding upon lower courts such as those presided over by magistrates and coroners, and are usually, but not necessarily, followed in subsequent High Court judgements. Decisions by the Appellate Courts (Court of Appeal and House of Lords) are binding on all lower courts and, although the House of Lords has a power to reverse a decision of its own, this is only invoked very rarely.

The range of factual situations that come before the courts is such that judges often have to decide cases in circumstances that have not been anticipated or considered by Parliament. Because a decision has to be made, the result is judge-made law (the 'common law'). As long-established legal principles are applied to the fresh legal dilemmas and challenges posed by modern society, the common law is subject to evolution and refinement, in a way consistent with historical decisions. The flexibility to respond to such novel situations is seen as one of the strengths of the common law.

The role of policy considerations in judicial decision-making

In determining how the law should develop, the courts are bound to be influenced by considerations of public and social policy, either in allowing claims where justice demands and to address a perceived ill, or to restrict liability where it is considered to have extended too far. An example is the recovery of damages for psychiatric injury where, in the absence of intervention by Parliament, the courts have devised a series of 'control mechanisms' to restrict the extent of liability and the cohort of potential claimants.[1-3]

Certain areas of the law (*e.g.* that relating to clinical negligence) have developed almost exclusively through caselaw. Others (*e.g.* concerning abortion) are set in a framework established by statute.

Statutory law

Superimposed upon common law are the provisions of statute. Statutes are Acts of Parliament brought into force after completion of a series of procedural steps, culminating in the grant of Royal Assent. Such parliamentary legislation may define an issue not previously subject to exploration in the courts, or it may consolidate principles established at common law. The courts are the final arbiter of the interpretation of legislation and can, therefore, have a significant effect on its application in practice. Only Parliament itself, however, can rescind or amend Acts of Parliament, by further legislation.

Many Acts create a power to delegate subsidiary decision-making to a designated minister, local authority or other official. This 'subordinate legislation' (*e.g.* Statutory Instrument or Regulations) can be effected swiftly when need arises, to make changes to detail as distinct from principle. If there are concerns that these delegated powers have been used improperly, application can be made for judicial review, whereby ministerial decisions are subject to review by the courts (*i.e.* the judiciary).

European Law

The *European Communities Act, 1972* requires that all provisions of European Union law intended to take direct effect in the UK shall do so. This means that when called upon to interpret UK statutes, the domestic courts must do so in conformity with EU law. Matters of conflict may be referred to the European Court of Justice, in Luxembourg. Once the European Court of Justice has given its decision on the specific point of law, the case is returned to the English courts for final determination in the light of the European ruling.[4]

The *Human Rights Act, 1998* incorporated into English law the European Convention for the Protection of Human Rights and Fundamental Freedoms (ECHR). The UK was an original signatory to the Convention in 1950 but did not incorporate its terms into domestic law at that time. Claimants can now assert a right under the Convention through the English courts, although the European Court of Human Rights, in Strasbourg, remains the final arbiter for those who remain dissatisfied.

The civil and criminal justice systems

The essential difference between a civil and a criminal offence is that the former arises from conflict between two or more individuals and is aimed at securing recompense, whereas the latter reflects conflict between an individual and society with a view to punishment. Minor criminal offences are dealt with in the Magistrates Court but matters of greater significance are heard in the Crown Court by a judge sitting with a jury selected at random from the electoral register.

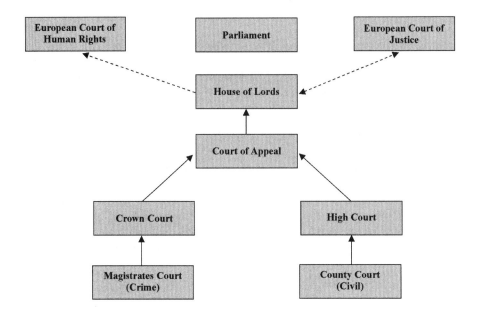

Civil cases at first instance are managed and heard, either in the County Court (claims for less than £50,000) or the High Court (for more serious or complex cases). Juries are no longer used in negligence claims and the small proportion of civil cases that go to trial are heard by a judge alone other than in exceptional circumstances. The Civil Procedure Rules (see Chapter 5) apply to both High Court and County Court actions.

Civil Appeals are heard by three Lord Justices in the Court of Appeal. Challenges on points of law or principle will be explored at appeal more readily than those on fact or discretion, which are only rarely overturned. This is because the judge at first instance has the benefit of taking evidence directly from the witnesses, whereas the Court of Appeal deals solely with the transcript.

Final appeals reach the House of Lords and require leave (permission), either from the Court of Appeal or House of Lords itself. Matters of exceptional significance are heard by a court of seven Law Lords, with lesser matters usually being dealt with by five. Appeal to the House of Lords arising from clinical negligence claims is infrequent and is used most often to clarify an important principle or to determine legal policy on controversial ethical issues.[5,6]

The purposes of the law

The law and legal system have a number of primary functions:

➣ to establish and define standards of acceptable behaviour

➣ to maintain those standards and punish 'offences'

➣ to facilitate easy, calm, ordered commercial relations, to enable trade and business

> to provide compensation – just recompense for injury
> to do justice and put right wrongs.

Above all, the 'rule of law' serves to promote civil order and to achieve the resolution of disputes without the use of force. The alternative is dissatisfaction, with the risk of civil strife.

The law in Scotland, Northern Ireland and other jurisdictions

English common law applies in England and Wales. It is similar in principle in Northern Ireland but there are some differences (*e.g.* in coroner's court proceedings). The law in Scotland is somewhat different in both structure and principle. Fortunately, the differences of principle between English and Scottish law relating to clinical negligence are minor and need not to be considered here. Appeal from the Scottish Courts is to the House of Lords and cases arising in Scotland can, therefore, contribute to shaping the law in England and Wales.[7]

Reference is occasionally made to cases decided in other common law jurisdictions (*e.g.* Canada, Australia, US and New Zealand). Such decisions are, however, only of persuasive rather than binding value and, in practice, reference to authority from another jurisdiction is only permitted where there is no similar or contrary authority on the same point from England and Wales.

Legislative basis for the regulation of health care

A plethora of statutes defines the components and organisation of the NHS, such that the legislative underpinning of healthcare is both complex and inaccessible. A consolidating NHS Act has been drafted by the Law Commission to bring all the relevant provisions into a single act. In the meantime, some of the most significant recent statutes are:

> *National Health Service Act, 1977*
  'It is the Secretary of State's duty to continue the promotion in England and Wales of a comprehensive health service designed to secure improvement – (a) in the physical and mental health of the people of those countries, and (b) in the prevention, diagnosis and treatment of illness, and for that purpose to provide or secure the effective provision of services in accordance with this Act. ... The services so provided shall be free of charge....'

> *NHS and Community Care Act, 1990*
  Encouraged 'care in the community', created NHS trusts and established GP Fundholding.

> *NHS Primary Care Act, 1997*
  Provided for the patient's right to choose their medical and dental practitioners – subject to the practitioners' consent.

> *Health Act, 1999*
  Abolished GP Fundholding, created Primary Care Trusts and the Commission for Health Improvement (CHI).

➤ *Health and Social Care Act, 2001*

> Complicated mix of provisions for financial funding of NHS Trusts, public–private partnerships, out-of-hours medical services, pharmacy dispensing, public involvement, establishing the Family Health Service Appeal Authority, etc.

➤ *NHS Reform and Healthcare Professions Act, 2002*

> Abolished Community Health Councils, established Strategic Health Authorities and the Council for Regulation of Healthcare Professionals.

➤ *Health and Social Care (Community Health and Standards) Act, 2003*

> Provided for the establishment of NHS Foundation Trusts and replaced CHI and the National Care Standards Commission with CHAI – now known as the Healthcare Commission.

Regulations governing the availability and prescribing of medicinal products are also enshrined in statute and so too are the powers to register and regulate the performance of medical practitioners. A number of other statutes apply to specific aspects of medical practice (*e.g.* assisted reproduction, abortion and tissue retention). In the recent past, the UK Government has responded to public concern about the NHS by establishing a number of new statutory authorities. These include the National Institute for Clinical Excellence (NICE), Commission for Health Care Audit and Improvement (the Healthcare Commission), National Patient Safety Agency (which registers accidents and near misses) and the National Clinical Assessment Authority (to supervise the performance of doctors who may be under-performing).

Sources of legal information

Law reports – referred to as 'authorities' – are published in a number of periodical series. Law reports may include a head-note or summary. These are not part of the official judgement and should be used cautiously. The national press, particularly *The Times* Law Reports, includes some detailed and authoritative reports which are accepted as legal authority if the case is not reported elsewhere.

Accepted abbreviations are used to identify law reports; those used here are explained in front of the Table of Cases. Case citations are used to identify individual cases and include the names of the parties and reference to the law report series in which it is published. The year of publication is often an essential identifying feature and is quoted in brackets []. The date precedes the abbreviation for the series, followed by the page number, often with a subsidiary reference to a particular passage in the judgement. The same case may be reported in several reports' series – leading to different citations. Since 2001, cases have been assigned neutral citations, which do not refer to any law report series.

Before relying on a reported decision, care must be taken to ensure that it has not been overturned on appeal or superseded by a subsequent decision from a higher court. Lawyers use specialist databases for this purpose. As in medicine, the key is to use up-to-date text books, keep abreast of developments as reported in professional journals and to discuss difficult cases and dilemmas with trusted colleagues or professional advisors.

Grouped reports of medical caselaw are available in the *Lloyd's Law Reports* (medical) series. Inquests are not reported formally but appeals arising from them appear in Justice of the Peace Reports and sometimes in other series as well.

Free Internet sources of legal authority and medicolegal information

Recent legislation is available without restriction on the Internet. Recent important judgements of the High Court and Appeal Courts are also posted on the Internet where they can be identified by name or court number. There are also a number of useful web-based sources of legal commentary.

www.opsi.gov.uk and www.hmso.gov.uk	Office of Public Sector Information – full text of UK legislation since 1988
www.courtservice.gov.uk	Access to recently decided cases
www.bailii.org	British and Irish Legal Information Institute – very comprehensive free source of case law from higher courts
www.nhsla.com/humanrights	National Health Service Litigation Authority Human Rights Information Service
www.parliament.the-stationery-office.co.uk	Decisions of the House of Lords – Parliamentary procedures and publications
www.dca.gov.uk	Department for Constitutional Affairs – information about legal procedure, Parliamentary Bills and legislation; links to other sources of legal information
www.lawreports.co.uk	Incorporated Council of Law Reporting; Daily Law Notes – free summaries of recent cases
www.ethox.org.uk	Teaching material on medical ethics and law
www.echr.coe.int	Decisions of the European Court of Human Rights
www.nhsla.com	National Health Service Litigation Authority – details of NHSLA risk management schemes, recent medicolegal cases and advice to clinicians

www.dh.gov.uk	Department of Health – source of official policy guidance
www.gmc-uk.org	General Medical Council – guidance, publications and details of disciplinary hearings
www.ethics-network.org.uk	The UK Clinical Ethics Network – links to articles on recent medicolegal/ ethical developments
http://www.hse.gov.uk	Health & Safety Executive website

Textbooks on medical law

A small number of long-established textbooks, usually referred to by the name of the original author, have status as legal authority and may be quoted in court. There are also 'casebooks' containing abstracts of reports on specific legal topics, often accompanied by useful and authoritative comment.

Brazier M. *Medicine, Patients and the Law*, 3rd edn, Penguin Books, 2003
> Accessible general text with broad coverage of medicolegal topics (560 pages)

Hockton A. *The Law of Consent to Medical Treatment*, Sweet & Maxwell, 2002
> Detailed review of consent law, with extensive source materials as appendices (300 pages)

Grubb A. (ed) *Principles of Medical Law*, 2nd edn. Oxford University Press 2004
> Authoritative reference book (1190 pages) – an annual update is published as a cumulative supplement

Matthews P. *Jervis on the Office and Duties of Coroners*, 12th edn. Sweet & Maxwell, 2002
> Detailed practitioners' text (925 pages) with regular supplements also available

Powers MJ, Harris N. (eds) *Clinical Negligence*, 3rd edn. Butterworths, 2000
> Reference book (1700 pages) – but an interesting mixture of commentary by lawyers and clinicians with chapters focused on individual medical specialities

Casebooks on medical law

Kennedy I, Grubb A.	*Medical Law: text and materials*, 3rd edn. Butterworths, 2000
Knapman P, Powers MJ.	*Sources of Coroners' Law*. Barry Rose, 1999
Maclean A,	*Briefcase on Medical Law*, 2nd edn. Cavendish Publishing, 2004

Nelson-Jones R & Burton F.   *Medical Negligence* Caselaw. 2nd edn.
Butterworths, 1995

Stauch M, Wheat K   *Sourcebook on Medical Law*, 3rd edn. Cavendish
Publishing, (Stauch, Tingle & Wheat) 2002

Relevant journals

➤ *The Journal of Clinical Risk*   Royal Society of Medicine Press.
(http://www.rsmpress.co.uk/cr.htm)

➤ *Medical Law Review*   (http://medlaw.oxfordjournals.org/)

➤ *Medico-legal Journal*   published quarterly for the Medico-legal
Society (www.medico-legalsociety.org.uk)

➤ *Journal of Medical Ethics*   (http://jme.bmjjournals.com/)

➤ *NHSLA Review and Journal*   available without charge on NHSLA
website – www.nhsla.com

References

1. *White v Chief Constable of South Yorkshire Police* [1999] 2 AC 455
   In one of a series of cases in the aftermath of the Hillsborough disaster, the House of Lords considered whether claims should be allowed for psychiatric injury arising from watching distressing events on television, and placed restrictions on the class of potential claimants, explicitly on grounds of public policy. 'No one...' said Lord Hoffmann '...can pretend that the existing law [in this area] is founded upon principle'.

2. *Rees v Darlington Memorial Hospital NHS Trust* [2003] UKHL 52
   In considering a case of negligent failed sterilisation, the House of Lords' decision re-affirmed the position it had taken in *Macfarlane (see ref. 6 below)* explicitly on policy grounds. The Courts will not weigh-up the costs of bringing up an unwanted 'normal healthy child', against the intangible joys, benefits and rewards of parenthood. A conventional sum of £15,000 is, however, to be awarded to reflect the interference with the patient's autonomy by way of the unwanted pregnancy.

3. *Dutton v Bognor Regis Urban District Council* [1972] 1 QB 373, 397
   In a claim for negligence in the surveying of a house, Lord Denning explained: *'This case is entirely novel. Never before has a claim been made against a council or its surveyor for negligence in passing a house... In previous times, when faced with a new problem, the judges have not openly asked themselves the question: what is the best policy for the law to adopt? But the question has always been there in the background... Nowadays we direct ourselves to considerations of policy... In short, we look at the relationship of the parties: and then say, as matter of policy, on whom the loss should fall.'*

4   Hip patient 'entitled to seek treatment abroad'. *The Times,* 16 December 2005

Challenge in the European Court of Justice (ECJ) to the procedure by which patients may obtain financial support from the NHS for treatment obtained in the European Union, but outside the UK. Case previously considered in the English High Court in *Watts v Bedford Primary Care Trust [2003] EWHC 2228 (Admin).* Following interpretation of European Law by the ECJ (*Watts [Freedom to Provide Services] [2006] EUECJ C-372/04 [16 May 2006]*) case returned to English courts for further consideration.   Court of Appeal decision pending.

5.   *Gillick v W Norfolk & Wisbech AHA* [1986] AC 112

An issue of social principle: is it acceptable to provide contraceptive advice to a child below 16 years without parental consent? Decision of the House of Lords formed the basis for defining the consensual capacity of children.

6.   *Airedale NHS Trust v Bland* [1993] 4 Med LR 39

Was it lawful to withdraw life-sustaining treatment from a patient in persistent vegetative state? Landmark House of Lords decision was careful to point out that each case should be considered individually.

7.   *Macfarlane & another v Tayside Health Board (Scotland)* [2000] UKHL 50

The pain and inconvenience of child-bearing arising from negligent failure of sterilisation are to be compensated but the costs of rearing the child are not recoverable. This House of Lords decision reversed earlier English caselaw.

2

Principles of negligence, duty and standard of care

Legal basis for claims arising from clinical practice

Civil claims may be founded in a number of areas of law, either separately or in combination.

Tort

'Tort' is the generic term for civil wrong-doing and is derived from the Latin *tortus*, twisted or wrong. 'Clinical negligence', a term used in preference to 'medical negligence' to encompass actions against all health professionals, is a sub-section of the law of tort. The legal criteria for a finding of negligence are: (i) the existence of a duty of care owed by one person or legal body to another; (ii) breach of that duty of care; and (iii) foreseeable injury occurring as a consequence of the breach. All three elements of the test must be fulfilled if the claimant is to succeed.[1]

Contract

Private medical practice generates claims founded on breach of contract as well as negligence.[2] A contract is an agreement creating obligations recognised and enforceable by law. It requires: (i) offer, (ii) acceptance, and (iii) consideration – the price for which the promise is bought.

No consideration passes directly between an NHS patient and the practitioner or treating hospital. There is, therefore, no legally enforceable, individual contract.[3] As a result, claims alleging wrongful medical practice within an NHS hospital are virtually always brought in tort.

At law, terms may be implied into contracts, even if they do not appear there, to the effect that a professional person undertakes to perform his duties with reasonable care and skill. The allegations of wrong-doing, either action or omission, cited in claims in tort or contract are often identical and typically relate to whether or not the services provided were of a reasonable standard.

Human rights

By virtue of *The Human Rights Act, 1998*, it is unlawful for UK public authorities to act in any way that is incompatible with rights protected under the European Convention of Human Rights. Allegations that such rights have been contravened have succeeded in the context of applications under the mental health legislation, in disciplinary proceedings against medical practitioners (see Chapter 8) in relation to treatment decisions concerning children (see Chapter 7) and concerning coroner's inquiries into deaths whilst under medical care (see Chapter 9).

Rationing and resource allocation

There is limited scope for individual patients to bring claims against public bodies where their service as a whole is considered unacceptably deficient.[4] In general, however, the courts are reluctant to interfere with decisions, taken in good faith, on the allocation of scarce resources.[5] 'Blanket bans' on a particular procedure have been challenged successfully,[6] as has a decision to close a specialist unit, albeit with criticism directed to the decision-making procedure rather than the decision itself.[7] Actions of this nature seek a remedy for alleged maladministration, not compensation for negligently inflicted personal injury. The appropriate legal process is, therefore, not an action in tort but Judicial Review.

In Judicial Review cases, the court is asked to assess whether a decision or action of a public body was lawful. The primary concern is whether the correct procedures were followed in the decision-making process, in particular whether:

- all relevant considerations were taken into account

- no irrelevant factors influenced the decision

- the administrative body acted within its proper powers

- any required public consultation took place; and

- the decision was not so unreasonable as to be illogical, perverse or irrational (*i.e.* beyond the range of responses open to a reasonable decision-maker).[8]

Other claims

The *Health Act, 1999* imposed for the first time, a statutory duty on Health Authorities, Primary Care Trusts and NHS Trusts to monitor and improve the quality of health care. Whilst the primary duty is to patients, the personal welfare of staff is included.[9] Statutory duties also arise from the provision of products to the public.[10]

Duty of care

The professional obligation of doctors to their patients suffices to found a common law duty of care. This commences at the point at which a 'duty relationship' (*e.g.* doctor/patient) is established, for example on acceptance of a referral.[4] Actions or decisions taken in the doctor/patient relationship may also affect others in addition to the patient and, in very limited circumstances, the doctor may also owe a duty to such third parties.[11–13] Concern over child welfare can lead to difficulty where there is apparent conflict between duties to parent and child. Safeguarding the best interests of the child is paramount.[14]

Occasionally, there are differences between professional and legal duties. If a patient suffers harm during the course of medical treatment, for example, there is a professional duty to explain what has happened.[15] There is, however, no freestanding legal duty of candour (see further Chapter 6). Equally, concerning 'good Samaritan' acts, there is a professional duty on doctors to offer anyone at risk whatever assistance could 'reasonably be expected' in an emergency, wherever it may arise (GMC *Good Medical Practice*, paragraph 9). There is, however, no legal duty to assist.[16]

Sometimes, a doctor's primary duty is to an individual or organisation other than the patient, for example, medical examinations for the purposes of employment or insurance. Here the doctor/patient relationship does not exist in conventional terms but the practitioner still has a duty to avoid causing harm to the patient and whether or not liability arises may depend on the nature of any error.[17]

Standard of care

In English law, the standard required of medical practitioners is determined by judicial analysis of relevant professional opinion. There may be more than one perfectly acceptable approach to any particular clinical situation and it is a defence to an allegation of negligence for a doctor to show that his actions were in accordance with practice accepted as proper by a responsible body of medical practitioners, skilled in that field.[18] This traditional '*Bolam*' test, is so named from the case in which the principle was enunciated.

Any medical opinion on which the court relies in assessing the standard of care must be 'reasonable'[19] and, whilst the court will be slow to reject the sincerely held views of distinguished experts, when experts conflict the judge may decide between them by assessing their credibility and rationality. To be considered acceptable, therefore, practice must be reasonably up-to-date[20] and formulated on the basis of a considered evaluation of the risks and benefits associated with a particular procedure and thus be capable of withstanding logical analysis.[21,22] It is accordingly not acceptable to practice in a certain way out of tradition, personal expediency or personal preference without an evidence base or reasonable grounds. Extreme or emergency situations may, however, justify the taking of risks that would otherwise be considered unacceptable.

The standard applied is not that of the most skilled specialist but that of the ordinarily, competent practitioner in the relevant field[23] and due consideration is given to the different standards which may apply to sub-specialties,[24] even if numerically small. Finally, and very importantly, the standard to be determined is that which applied at the time of the events in question, not after the event or at the time of Trial;[25] a decision is not negligent merely because it turns out to be wrong, so long as it was reasonable at the time that it was taken.

In some instances, guidelines or protocols are cited as a means of defining proper standards. Important though such guidelines are, legally as well as in practice, they are better considered as indicative of an accepted course of practice, or even best practice, rather than the final arbiter of acceptable professional standards. Failure to follow guidelines is not necessarily negligent,[26] but it may be necessary to show good reason for the course of action taken.

In very limited circumstances, responsibility for harm suffered by a patient is determined on a 'strict liability' basis. In such cases, it is not necessary for the patient to show that there was any 'fault', or that care was substandard, merely that the injury was casually related to the medical activity or product concerned.[10]

Inexperienced staff

Although the court may sympathise with a junior doctor called upon to undertake tasks beyond his competence, the standard to be applied is that of a competent professional capable of working in the relevant field.[27] Hospitals are expected to have in place systems and staff with sufficient experience and expertise to ensure that an appropriate standard of care is provided to all patients[28,29] and junior clinical staff should call for assistance before undertaking a task or dealing with a situation beyond their competence or experience.

Vicarious liability

Employers are vicariously responsible for the actions of their staff acting in the course of their employment. Historically, however, 'health authorities' were not held responsible for the errors of medical staff working on their premises, on the grounds that the authorities were not qualified to dictate what appropriate medical treatment should be. Since 1990, however, NHS hospitals have carried financial responsibility for the clinical errors of medical as well as all other employed staff.[30] It is, therefore, now usual for hospital trusts to be named as the defendant to claims in clinical negligence. Accordingly, employing authorities are entitled, and expected, to have protocols, guidelines and procedures in place to ensure that appropriate and approved treatment is provided to patients. At present, actions against general practitioners still lie against the individual doctor.[31] Private practitioners are either pursued individually or are identified as a co-defendant with a private hospital, depending on the individual contractual arrangements and the allegations made.

Suggested further reading

Newsletters of the NHSLA Human Rights Information Service can be accessed at – http://www.nhsla.com/Publications/

HSG (96) 48 'NHS Indemnity – Arrangements for Clinical Negligence Claims in the NHS' may be found under the 'publications and statistics' section of the Department of Health website at – www.dh.gov.uk

Goldberg R. Paying for bad blood: strict product liability after the Hepatitis C litigation. Med Law Rev 2002; **10**: 165–200

References

1. *Barnett v Chelsea & Kensington HMC [1969] 1QB 428; 2 WLR 422*
   Casualty officer declined to attend three night-watchmen who were vomiting after drinking tea; one died later from arsenical poisoning. Claim failed. Breach of duty established but no causation – man would have died anyway.

2. Dyer C. Triplets' parents win right to damages for extra child. *BMJ* 2000; **321**: 1305
   Successful claim in contract. Three embryos rather than the agreed two were implanted. Parents could claim for cost of additional child.

3. *Reynolds v The Health First Medical Group [2000] Lloyd's Rep Med 240*
   Attempt to circumvent the rules of negligence by asserting a contractual obligation between GP and patient, with NHS capitation fee as consideration. Claim struck-out: the relationship between doctor and patient is statutory not contractual.

4. *Kent v Griffiths, Roberts and London Ambulance Service [2000] Lloyd's Rep Med 109*
   Asthmatic patient suffered respiratory arrest and brain damage during inexplicable prolonged wait for an emergency ambulance. Judgement, solely against the LAS, was upheld on Appeal. The LAS owed a duty of care to the individual patient once the 999 call had been received and dispatch of an ambulance had been promised. LAS as a body owed a duty to respond within a reasonable period, which it had failed to do.

5. *R v Cambridge HA ex parte B (A Minor) [1995] 6 Med LR 250*
   Decision not to provide unproven treatment for relapse of leukaemia in a child. 'Difficult and agonising decisions have to be made as to how a limited budget is best allocated to the maximum advantage of the maximum number of patients. That is not a Judgement which the court can make.'

6. *NW Lancs HA v A, D & G. [1999] Lloyd's Rep Med 399*
   Policy not to fund gender re-assignment surgery, other than in very exceptional cases, was 'effectively a blanket ban'. Rationing accepted as inevitable but must be based on proper assessment of clinical need.

7. *R v NW Thames RHA et al ex parte Daniels [1993] 4 Med LR 364*
   Health Authority erred in failing to consult interested parties before closing a bone marrow transplant unit but no public law remedy was granted because none would have benefited the applicant.

8. *R (on the application of Rogers) v Swindon NHS Primary Care Trust & Secretary of State for Health [2006] EWCA Civ 392*
   Judicial review of PCT policy concerning the provision of Herceptin to patients with early breast cancer. The policy made allowance for treatment of women, meeting certain clinical eligibility criteria, 'in exceptional circumstances'. There was, however, no reasonable basis on which to determine what those exceptional circumstances might be or how to distinguish between patients in the eligible group. The Court of Appeal concluded that the policy was accordingly irrational and, therefore, unlawful. Notably, the court would have found 'nothing arbitrary or irrational' about an approach that took into account financial constraints and balanced cost considerations against the individual circumstances of the patient, but in this case the PCT policy treated financial considerations as irrelevant.

9. *Ogden v Airdale HA [1996] 7 Med LR 153*
   Faulty working conditions permitted radiographer to become sensitised to X-

ray chemicals, developing asthma. Damages awarded for his condition, loss of earnings, loss of chosen career and loss of job security. The employer's duty to its staff arises not only in negligence but also under statute (*e.g. Health and Safety at Work Act, 1974*). See also 'Hospital Trust faces sentence for staff death' (*The Guardian*, 18 April 2005) - South West London and St George's Mental Health Trust pleaded guilty to neglect contributing to death of a healthcare assistant who was killed by a patient.

10. *A and Ors v The National Blood Authority and Others [2001] EWHC QB 446*
   Successful claim by patients infected with hepatitis C during blood transfusion. The Authority was held responsible under the terms of the *Consumer Protection Act, 1987* in compliance with the *European Union Product Liability Directive* of 1985. See also, '£750,000 award for blood error' (*The Times*, 21 September 2005) – compensation award to patient who contracted a variant of HIV from infected blood.

11. *Goodwill v British Pregnancy Advisory Service [1996] 2All ER 161*
   Patient was negligently assured that his vasectomy had been successful. Whilst a duty of care was owed to the male patient, no duty was owed to his potential future sexual partners. No duty was owed to the plaintiff, who was not the man's girlfriend at the time of surgery, notwithstanding that in reliance on the erroneous advice she used no contraceptive precautions and became pregnant.

12. *Palmer v Tees HA, Hartlepool & East Durham NHS Trust [1999] Lloyds Rep Med 351*
   Psychotic patient murdered a child and mutilated her body a year after hospital discharge. Alleged to have told staff of sexual feelings towards children and that a child would be murdered. Claim on behalf of child and mother struck out – there was insufficient proximity between the hospital and an unknown victim to found a duty of care.

13. 'Sister who saw killing wins record trauma sum', *The Times*, 5 November 2001
   When a dangerously ill psychiatric patient was released to go home, he killed his mother and then himself. The Trust admitted liability for the post-traumatic stress disorder caused to the patient's sister.

14. *JD & Others v East Berks Community NHS Trust [2005] UKHL 23*
   The Court of Appeal held that, in some circumstances, health professionals owe a duty of care to a child when investigating suspicions of abuse. House of Lords confirmed that health professionals investigating suspected child abuse do not owe a further duty of care to the parents or others suspected of carrying out the abuse, if the investigation was carried out in good faith. Although the parents have a right to respect for their family life and protection from unwarranted intrusion, safeguarding the child's interests must be paramount.

15. General Medical Council. *Good Medical Practice*, 2001 (Good Communication - paras 22,23)
   Sets out the duty to explain what has happened when an adverse incident occurs and a patient suffers harm.

16. *Church of Jesus Christ of Later Day Saints (Great Britain) v Yorkshire Fire and Civil Defence Authority [1997] 2 All ER 865*
   In the absence of some special relationship or undertaking, the rescuer is not liable for failing to effect a rescue. If assistance is offered, there is no liability for negligence in the rescue attempts, unless that negligence makes the situation worse and causes more damage than would have occurred in any event.

17. *Kapfunde v Abbey National & Dr D Daniel [1999] 2 Lloyd's Rep Med 48*
   Occupational Health report commissioned by potential employer was adverse

to claimant's application for employment. No duty of care owed by practitioner to potential employee but see also *R v Croydon HA [1998] Lloyd's Rep Med 44* – failure to diagnose pulmonary hypertension on a pre-employment chest x-ray. Breach of duty admitted by the radiologist.

18. *Bolam v Friern Hospital Management Committee [1957] 1 WLR 583*

Claimant suffered fractures during ECT administered without muscle relaxants, a technique endorsed at the time by a 'responsible body of medical opinion'. Test for breach of duty set out by J McNair in directions to jury.

19. *Kennedy v Liverpool Women's Hospital NHS Trust (16 December 2004) MLC 1285*

Claim based on delay in detecting problems in labour. The judge concluded that the views of the eminent expert for the defence were '…not reasonable or respectable … for whatever reason his opinions are not objective and unbiased'. '…the level of care … was unacceptable, probably because the department was simply too busy to cope. The midwives were left to do their best with virtually no guidance or advice from the doctors.' Unsurprisingly in the circumstances the claimant succeeded.

20. Crawford v Board of Governors of Charing Cross Hospital (1953), *The Times* 8 December, CA

During urological surgery, a patient was positioned in such a way that he suffered brachial plexus injury, resulting in permanent weakness in the arm. Although the position was standard, an article in *The Lancet* 6 months earlier had warned of the danger. It was not negligent that the anaesthetist had not read and acted upon the article. Whilst there is a duty to be reasonably up-to-date, doctors are not expected to be aware of every latest research finding.

21. *Bolitho v City & Hackney HA [1997] UKHL 46*

Negligent failure to attend a child's respiratory crisis. Court is not necessarily bound by expert opinion. Support by distinguished experts will usually demonstrate reasonableness of an action but if, in rare cases, expert opinion is incapable of withstanding logical analysis, judge is entitled to find it is not reasonable or responsible.

22. *Hucks v Cole [1993] 4 Med LR 393*

Despite expert evidence that some doctors would not have given the patient antibiotics, the Court of Appeal found a GP negligent for not prescribing Penicillin to a patient suffering from a condition which could lead to puerperal fever. The reasons for failing to take precautionary action were considered unreasonable and failed to stand up to judicial analysis when weighed against the risks which could have been easily and inexpensively avoided.

23. *Knight v Home Office [1990] 3 All ER 237*

A general prison doctor is not expected to attain the standard of a specialist in psychiatric care.

24. *Defreitas v O'Brien & Another [1993] 4 Med LR 281*

Exploratory spinal surgery in absence of clear clinical or radiological indications to operate. Spinal surgeons deemed to form a category of specialism distinct from other orthopaedic and neurosurgeons.

25. *Roe v Ministry of Health [1954] 2 WLR 915*

Paraplegia following spinal anaesthesia; ampoules stored in phenol which leaked through invisible cracks in the glass – a risk that was unknown at the time. The claim failed: 'we must not look at a 1947 accident with 1954 spectacles' per Lord Denning.

26. *A v North East London Strategic Health Authority [2005] EWHC 950*

    Claimant suffered brain damage, which would have been avoided by earlier caesarean section delivery. Although the doctor's actions were not in compliance with the hospital protocol, they were not negligent and the claim failed.

27. *Wilsher v Essex AHA [1988] AC 1074*

    Failure by junior doctor in special care baby unit to recognise misplacement of umbilical artery catheter, leading to treatment on basis of venous blood gas results as if they were arterial. Inexperience is no defence to negligence – a driver having obtained a driving licence is expected to drive safely even though newly qualified. On the other hand, 'Full allowance must be made for the fact that certain aspects of treatment may have to be carried out in what one witness called … battlefield conditions. An emergency may overburden the available resources, and, if an individual is faced by circumstances to do too many things at once, the fact that he does one of them incorrectly should not lightly be taken as negligence' per LJ Mustill.

28. *Bull v Devon AHA [1993] 4 Med LR 117*

    Birth asphyxia in second twin. Failure to attend obstetric emergency. Health Authority liable for failure to provide and implement efficient system for alerting appropriate staff on-call to an impending emergency. See also *Robertson v Nottingham HA [1997] 8 Med LR 1*. Brain damaged infant – fetal distress before onset of labour. Health Authority had a duty to establish proper systems of care and can be liable for a 'systems failure' resulting in communication breakdown.

29. 'Hospital in dock over MRSA deaths', *The Times* 1 November 2005

    NHS Trust pleaded guilty to breach of Section 3 of the *Health & Safety at Work Act, 1974* (HSWA), which obliges all employers to operate systems of work in a way, so far as is reasonably practicable, to prevent avoidable risks to the health and safety of employees and members of the public, including patients. Allegation that inadequate supervision of two junior doctors, leading to death of a patient, represented a breach of statutory duty. The two doctors had already been convicted of manslaughter by gross negligence. Also, in 1998, Norfolk & Norwich Healthcare NHS Trust was fined £38,000 for a breach of Section 3 HSWA following the death of a patient from an air embolism during cardiac angiography. HSE's investigation identified the lack of a safe system of work for operating the automated syringe used to inject the contrast medium.

30. *Health Service Circular – HC (89) 34*

    Confirmed that, as of 1 April 1990, financial responsibility for clinical negligence claims rested with the employing NHS authority. Useful background information and explanation of the subsequent arrangements is contained in *NHS Indemnity – Arrangements for Clinical Negligence Claims in the NHS*' (at http://www.nhsla.com/Publications/ under 'Claims Publications').

31. *Strategic Health Authority Flyer* (at http://www.nhsla.com/Publications under 'Claims Publications')

    The NHSLA anticipates the potential for Primary Care Trusts to be held liable for claims arising from Primary Care. See also *Gooden & Others v Kent & Medway SHA 8 July 2004 MLC 1263* – NHS patients, who alleged that their GP had assaulted them, had an arguable claim against the Strategic Health Authority as successor to the GP's employing authority.

3

Foreseeability and causation

The burden and standard of proof

It is incumbent on the claimant in a civil case to establish his case on the balance of probabilities.[1,2] First, the facts must be established and thereafter the successful claimant must demonstrate all three elements of negligence – existence of a duty, breach of that duty, and foreseeable injury occurring as a result. The facts may be a matter of contention between the parties, particularly if the medical notes are inconclusive. If there is conflict and the matter reaches court, the judge is responsible for making a determination of 'fact' in the light of the evidence presented and his view of the credibility of the witnesses.

The third limb of the test for negligence is itself tripartite. The claimant must establish: (i) foreseeability, (ii) injury, and (iii) occurrence as a result of the breach of the duty of care.

Foreseeability

Complications arising in the course of medical treatment are sometimes wholly unexpected. In legal terms, however, an injury is deemed to be a foreseeable consequence of the negligent act if damage of that general nature can be foreseen. For example, although anterior spinal artery syndrome would not be cited as a specific risk of induced hypotension during anaesthesia, injury caused by under-perfusion of major organs is a foreseeable consequence.[3] In practice, it must be accepted that it is foreseeable that most medical duties, if performed negligently, may cause adverse effects either localised or systemic.

Injury

Actions in negligence are brought to secure compensation for harm suffered as a result of a wrongful act. Without an injury causally related to the tort, there is no basis for a claim. This contrasts with actions in battery where unlawful (*i.e.* non-consensual) touching warrants compensation, whether or not 'injury' has occurred as a consequence. Similarly, failure to respect a patient's right to autonomy, under Article 8 of the European Convention of Human Rights, may give rise to an award of compensation, even though the outcome would probably have been the same in any event.[4]

Injury which founds a claim for damages can be physical, mental or economic. However, the courts are more willing to compensate physical rather than mental or economic injury. The victim of a negligent act who suffers psychiatric injury in conjunction with physical injury, or in circumstances where personal injury of some kind is reasonably foreseeable, is deemed a 'primary victim' and is entitled to compensation.[5,6] Conversely, a claimant who suffers psychiatric injury from witnessing or learning of the consequences of negligent harm to another is deemed a 'secondary victim' and can only recover damages if able to overcome a number of restrictions. They must show:

➢ A close emotional bond with the primary victim.

➢ That psychiatric illness resulted from sudden appreciation by sight or sound of shocking circumstances proximate in time and place to the negligence or its immediate aftermath.

➢ That it was reasonably foreseeable that an onlooker of normal foreseetitude would suffer mental distress resulting in psychiatric illness.[7,8]

Economic loss which is consequent upon negligently inflicted physical or mental injury, for example loss of earnings or the cost of care, is recoverable. However, the courts are reluctant to award damages for pure economic loss without accompanying physical injury.

Causation of injury

An adverse outcome from medical treatment, even when unexpected, does not suffice to establish a finding of clinical negligence. There must be a causal link with a breach of duty. This means that it is necessary for the claimant to establish that the adverse outcome would not have occurred in any event as a result of the natural progression of disease or treatment carried out to an appropriate standard. The claimant must show, on the balance of probabilities, that their injury would not have occurred 'but for' the negligence.

The requirement to prove a causal link between adverse outcome and breach of duty often presents an insuperable hurdle to the claimant bringing an action in clinical negligence. Many patients have difficulty understanding why their claim has failed when breach of duty is provable or even admitted. However, the claimant can succeed in full provided he can show that the negligence probably made a 'material contribution' to the outcome – in other words was more than *de minimis*.[9,10] In very exceptional cases, the courts will discount the sum awarded in compensation to reflect contributory negligence by the patient.[11]

Injury caused by failure to act

Here, the court is faced with a hypothetical situation: what would have been the outcome had there not been a negligent failure to act? In some cases, this requires evaluation of the natural progression of untreated disease and, after hearing expert evidence, the judge will make a finding of 'fact' – legal fact – as to what would have occurred but for the negligence.

The possibility of a future adverse outcome arising as a consequence of negligence may be taken into account in the assessment of damages (see Chapter 4). In determining the causation of past events, however, the legal process is 'all or none'. If it is determined that the adverse outcome would probably (i.e. more than 50% likelihood) have been avoided, but for the negligence, the claim succeeds in full with no discount for lack of certainty. If, on the other hand, the adverse outcome would probably have occurred in any event, then the claim fails outright.[12] This approach can appear arbitrary or unjust particularly when, through negligence, a patient has lost a significant chance of a cure or better recovery. The House of Lords has accordingly considered whether a claimant should be entitled to recover damages for the loss of a chance of less than 50% in proportion to the magnitude of the lost opportunity. By a 3:2 majority this proposition was rejected. It was considered relevant that the 'rule' works both ways and sometimes to the benefit of claimants.[13]

Difficulty has arisen where negligent failure to act does not have agreed consequences. Thus, if a practitioner negligently fails to attend a patient, the court must determine what that individual practitioner would have done if properly attending and, thereafter, whether that would have been in accordance with reasonable medical practice. It is no defence to argue that the outcome would have been the same even if the practitioner had attended the patient, because he would have been further negligent in again failing to act.[14]

Res ipsa loquitur - 'The thing speaks for itself'

This aphorism is merely a means of drawing an inference of negligence, on the balance of probabilities, where no other explanation is tenable. Although the burden of proof (to demonstrate his case) rests with the claimant, there are circumstances that give rise to a *prima facie* case of negligence. An obvious example is a retained instrument following surgical procedure. The defendant may rebut the presumption of negligence if he can offer a plausible, non-negligent explanation. It may also be possible to refute the inference of negligence by satisfying the judge that proper care was exercised or that the adverse outcome is impossible to explain in the light of current knowledge.[15] The stronger the evidence in support of the claimant, however, the greater the need for the defendant to produce convincing evidence or arguments that negligence did not occur.

Where the alleged negligence relates to assessment of physical evidence (*e.g.* X-rays, scans and pathology slides), in practice it can be extremely difficult to defend cases in which the passage of time has demonstrated that images or appearances were incorrectly interpreted, either as 'false negative' or 'false positive'. Although the standard *'Bolam'* approach applies, at times it can appear that the burden of proof has been reversed and the defendant is presumed negligent unless he can demonstrate otherwise.[16,17] There is a risk that over-cautious or 'defensive' medical practice may result as a consequence, with greater equivocation over results interpretation and reporting and more investigation 'just in case'. Whether medicine practised in this way results in benefit to patients, or exposes them to the risks of unnecessary investigation or treatment, is a moot point.[18]

Suggested further reading

Clinical Negligence: A very brief guide for clinicians. On the NHSLA website (www.nhsla.com/Publications/) under 'Claims Publications'

Faulks E. The Kent and Canterbury litigation. *Clin Risk* 2000; **6**: 153–156 (Commentary on the cervical screening litigation and the difficulties faced by the Courts in applying principles of negligence to cases of false negative and false positive results)

References

1. *Ratcliffe v Plymouth & Torbay HA et al [1998] Lloyd's Rep Med 162*
   Unexplained neurological defect after spinal anaesthesia. Court satisfied on balance of probabilities that proper care had been exercised and the claim failed.

2. *Wilsher v Essex AHA [1988] AC 1074*
   Retinopathy of prematurity occurred after negligent exposure to high concentrations of oxygen. Plaintiff failed to establish that oxygen toxicity, as distinct from other possible causes, was responsible in part or at all.

3. *Hepworth v Kerr [1995] 6 Med LR 139*
   Anterior spinal artery thrombosis attributed to excessive and unduly prolonged induced hypotension during general anaesthesia. Injury was but a variant of the foreseeable and within the risk created by the negligence.

4. *Chester v Afshar [2004] UKHL 41*
   A spinal surgeon negligently failed to warn his patient of the risk of cauda equina nerve damage during spinal surgery. In a controversial decision, the House of Lords decided that damages should be awarded, even though the patient would have elected to have the surgery in any event, albeit at a later date. The injury to be compensated was to the patient's right to autonomy, which had been breached.

5. *AB v Tameside and Glossop HA [1997] 8 Med LR91*
   Defendants conceded that they owed a duty of care to break bad news in a way that reduced the risk of psychiatric injury arising as a result. Sending letters through the post advising patients that they may have been exposed to HIV without arrangements for a readily accessible 'help-line' was subject to criticism.

6. *Farell v Avon Health Authority [2001] Lloyds Rep Med 458*
   A father was mistakenly informed that his son had died and was given a dead baby to hold. His child was in fact alive, but he was awarded damages for post-traumatic stress disorder.

7. *North Glamorgan NHS Trust v Walters [2002] EWCA Civ 1792*
   The hospital admitted that the claimant's child had died as a consequence of negligent treatment. During that treatment, the claimant, whilst resident in hospital with her sick son, woke to find him having a fit. His subsequent

transfer, treatment and demise, although extending over two days, were considered by the Court of Appeal to be a single shocking event so as to give rise to a claim for psychiatric injury.

8. *Ward v Leeds Teaching Hospitals NHS Trust [2004] EWCA 2106*

The claimants daughter died 48 hours after routine dental surgery. The judge held that, in the hospital context, death does not give rise to a claim for nervous shock unless accompanied by wholly exceptional circumstances in some way as to shock and horrify. This case demonstrates the need for good post-error care – keeping the relative aware of the gravity of the medical condition and avoiding exposure to shocking sights without due warning.

9. *Bonnington Castings Ltd v Wardlaw [1956] AC 613*

Silicosis attributable to both negligent and non-negligent exposure to dust. Negligence made a material contribution and, although unable to demonstrate there would have been no injury but for the negligence, claimant succeeded.

10. *Fairchild v Glenhaven Funeral Services [2002] UKHL 22*

House of Lords decision allowing claim brought by executrix of estate of deceased who developed lung cancer after exposure to asbestos while working for a variety of employers. It was not necessary to prove which of many exposures was responsible, since there was no scientific way to do so. Responsibility for the disease should be apportioned between the employers in proportion to the degree to which they had exposed the deceased to asbestos. (*Barker v Corus [UK] Plc [2006] UKHL 20*)

11. *Beverley Pidgeon v Doncaster Health Authority [2002] Lloyd's Rep Med 130*

Negligent failure correctly to identify an abnormal cervical smear was followed by a prolonged period without follow-up because the claimant repeatedly failed to heed medical advice that further checks were due, despite acknowledging she understood the importance of the test. A successful claim was brought after she developed invasive cervical cancer, but damages were reduced by two-thirds to reflect her contributory negligence. See also *Badger v Ministry of Defence (MOD) [2005] EWHC 2941*. Where a claimant should 'reasonably' have known of the risks of smoking, the compensation paid to his widow was reduced accordingly. Mr Badger contracted asbestosis and lung cancer after 33 years work in a dockyard. Although the MOD accepted primary liability, damages were reduced by 20% since 'it was reasonably foreseeable by a reasonably prudent man that, if he smoked, he risked damaging his health'.

12. *Hotson v East Berks AHA [1987] AC 750*

Delayed diagnosis of slipped epiphysis. There was a 75% likelihood that avascular necrosis would have occurred in any event and, at first instance, 25% of full damages was awarded to represent the lost chance. The damages award was reversed on appeal. The claim failed because an adverse outcome was more likely than not in any event.

13. *Greg v Scott [2005] UKHL 2*

GP negligently failed to refer patient with a suspicious lump to hospital. By the time the diagnosis of cancer was made, after a nine-month delay, the patient's prospects of 10-year survival had fallen from 42% to 25%. The claimant unsuccessfully sought damages for the 17% reduction in his chances of survival. Damages were denied by the House of Lords, since the claimant could not show, on the balance of probabilities, that his outcome would have been materially different 'but for' the negligence. Either way it was the cancer that was probably responsible for his reduced life expectancy. If the Courts were to adopt a policy of awarding damages in proportion to the provable loss, this would, thought Baroness Hale, have a detrimental effect on the majority of claimants who currently achieve full recovery having proved their case on the balance of probabilities. 'This would surely be a case of two steps forward and three steps back for the great majority of straightforward personal injury cases'. 'A "more likely than not" approach to causation suits both sides'.

14. *Bolitho v City & Hackney HA [1998] AC 232 and [1998] Lloyd's Rep Med 26*
    Failure to attend child with croup who finally sustained brain damage following a respiratory arrest. House of Lords confirmed the tests to be applied to determine consequence of a failure to act: what would the Practitioner have done if she had attended (*i.e.* would she have intubated) and what should the practitioner have done?

15. *Fish v Kapur [1948] 2All ER 176*
    A dentist dislocated his patient's jaw extracting a tooth. It was held that the injury could have occurred even if there had been no negligence. The claimant had not proved negligence on the balance of probabilities and *res ipsa loquitur* did not apply.

16. *Penny v East Kent Health Authority [1999] EWCA Civ 3005*
    Cervical screening had resulted in false-negative reports, with consequent delay in diagnosis/detection of cervical cancer. Cytoscreeners should not have given a negative result unless they could say with 'absolute confidence' that there was no abnormality.

17. *Lillywhite & Anor v University College London Hospitals NHS Trust [2005] EWCA Civ 1466*
    An 18-week antenatal scan was interpreted as normal but following birth part of the brain was found to be absent. By a 2:1 majority the Court of Appeal found an eminent Professor of Obstetrics negligent for failing to identify fetal abnormalities on the scan, notwithstanding that two other specialists had also failed to spot abnormalities. The mother's claim was based on the premise that she would have opted for an abortion had the abnormality been identified. Where there is a *prima facie* case of negligence, there is a 'heavy burden on (the defendant) to reconcile his incorrect conclusions with the exercise of all reasonable care and skill'. Appeal to House of Lords pending.

18. Tribe D, Korgaonkar G. The impact of litigation on patient care: an enquiry into defensive medical practices. *Prof Negligence* 1991; 7: 1

4

Financial considerations: compensation and costs

The outcome of a successful claim in negligence is an award of damages, a payment made to compensate the claimant for injury and its consequences. The intention is to restore the claimant, so far as money is able, to the position he would have been in but for the negligent act. Although some claimants apparently pursue legal action to obtain an explanation or apology, litigation cannot require such an outcome and monetary compensation is the only remedy available to the courts in this context.[1]

In respect to actions against the NHS, there is a conflict between the need to compensate an individual harmed by negligent medical treatment and the requirement to ensure that limited resources are preserved to provide high-quality care to all. More broadly, there must be a balance between adequate compensation for the individual and the cost of insurance to society as a whole. Concern has arisen, therefore, due to the rising cost of damages awards and associated legal costs.[2]

The size of the damages award (quantum) reflects the injury to the claimant and bears no relationship to the perceived or actual magnitude of any wrong-doing, although very occasionally an award is enhanced to reflect injury to the claimant's feelings or pride, or because of the defendant's unacceptable behaviour.[3] Punitive or 'aggravated damages' are deemed inappropriate in claims for negligence because of conflict with the principle of compensation, but they have been awarded for the tort of trespass to the person.[4] By contrast, damages for negligence in the US can include a punitive element and the awards are consequently higher.

Two types of damages are routinely awarded in negligence claims – general and special damages.

General damages

This is the sum awarded for pain, suffering and loss of amenity attributable to the injury. The 'value' of such items is highly subjective but damages' awards are based upon Judicial Studies Board Guidelines which are updated regularly and which set a range from within which awards for a particular injury are selected. Complete loss of vision in one eye with reduced vision in the other, for example, attracts general damages between £35,000 and £58,000. Caselaw is used to determine where in the range any individual case falls. This approach permits some consistency in the awards for like injuries but also allows for variation to reflect differences in the impact on individuals with similar injuries.

Special damages

These are losses which are attributable to the negligently caused injury and which are specific to the individual. Past losses such as reduced earnings, or equipment or travel costs can be calculated reasonably accurately whereas future losses are hypothetical and more contentious.

Future losses – the concept of multiplier and multiplicand

Serious injury can have repercussions for an individual and his family, which persist throughout and beyond his life-time. The totality of the loss is determined at the time of trial or settlement and traditionally the entire sum of damages is then available, either directly to the adult claimant of sound mind, or within the safe-keeping of the court for the benefit of minors and those of unsound mind. This 'accelerated receipt' means the claimant has the immediate benefit of funds which, but for the injury, would have taken a life-time to acquire (earn) or to require (care costs). Invested wisely, these funds increase in value in excess of inflation and an allowance must, therefore, be made to offset this benefit. Unpredictable variables and uncertainties for the individual must also be acknowledged when calculating, at any one time, what losses or needs may arise perhaps many years in the future. For this reason, the legal process has developed the concept of multiplier and multiplicand.

(i) The **multiplicand** is the anticipated annual net value of each element of future loss or expense, based on figures current at the date of trial.

(ii) The **multiplier** is the number of years over which the loss or expense is expected to occur, offset to allow for accelerated receipt and the uncertainties of predicting an individual's future.

The size of award for 'future losses' in cases of on-going permanent disability is affected by the calculation of life expectancy, which may, therefore, be a hotly contested issue between litigating parties. The court may have to assess the claimant's prognosis based on actuarial tables and expert opinion. The cost of providing on-going care is also determined by reference to expert opinion from diverse care therapists, employment experts and forensic accountants. There is often a very striking difference between the value of the claim as calculated by the opposing legal teams. Much time, effort and legal expense are then invested in resolving the differences and some cases go to trial solely for the court to decide quantum, even when liability has been determined or admitted.[5]

Structured settlements/periodic payments

In some cases, the estimation of life expectancy has proved to be wildly inaccurate, resulting either in 'over compensation' of a claimant who dies shortly thereafter, or 'under compensation' for the claimant who outlives the fund available to pay for his on-going care needs. To mitigate against such circumstances, the *Courts Act, 2003* requires that in every case in which a court awards damages for personal injury, it must consider whether the award should be made by way of periodic payments (*i.e.* X amount [to increase in line with the Retail Prices Index] over Y years) – whether with the agreement of the parties or not.

Provisional damages

The consequences of injury are not always immediately apparent. Some allowance for future deterioration may be made by including an additional sum to reflect the magnitude and significance of the risk of such deterioration (*e.g.* epilepsy after head injury). Alternatively, provisional damages can be awarded provided there is a real chance that at some future date the claimant will, as a result of the negligent act, develop some serious disease or suffer some serious deterioration in their condition. This allows initial compensation for the existing injury, coupled with a right, fixed by the court for a specified period, to claim further recompense if the predicted adverse future development does indeed occur.

Some specific elements of loss

Some heads of claim are easy to identify, such as loss of earnings, pension rights or a requirement for new or adapted housing to accommodate the needs of a disabled person. High-earning claimants secure far higher awards than those with low or no income because, without the negligent injury, they and their families would have enjoyed the benefits of the higher income. The purpose of the award is to compensate them for their loss.

If there is no measurable and predictable earnings loss, a claim may be allowed for disadvantage on the labour market (a *Smith v Manchester* award) where future career prospects may be compromised. The future losses of children are estimated from national average earnings in careers comparable to those of their parents or siblings. Such awards are never high because there is a large element of accelerated receipt and the loss is of a chance, not of a defined achievement.

Fatal accidents give rise to claims on behalf of the estate of the deceased (*Law Reform [Miscellaneous Provisions] Act, 1934*) and those financially dependent on the deceased at the time of death (*Fatal Accidents Act, 1976*). In addition to any proven individual losses, close relatives (spouses, civil partners[6] and parents of children less than 18 years) are entitled to a statutory bereavement award, currently £10,000. However, such an award is not triggered by death *in utero*, even if occurring as a consequence of negligence, and is, therefore, not recoverable following still-birth.

Possible future developments

Reduction in the costs of quantum assessment has been achieved by the increasing use of single experts to advise on matters of quantum, either jointly instructed by defendants and claimants, or appointed by the court. A more controversial proposal is the abolition of the statutory provision[7] that permits claimants to recover the costs of future medical treatment and services privately without reference to availability on the NHS or from local authorities.[8]

In October 2005, the *NHS Redress Bill* was published. If enacted, this would provide the Secretary of State with the power to establish an NHS Redress Scheme for clinical negligence claims up to a value of £20,000. The Scheme would be an alternative to litigation, aimed to reduce the expenditure on legal costs. Notably, healthcare providers would be required to review incidents as they occur and to refer cases to the scheme, with no onus on the patient to initiate a claim. Consequently, it is anticipated that if implemented, the Scheme will see the number of claims against the NHS rise by up to 43%.[9]

Funding litigation

Litigation is costly. Claims in clinical negligence are among the most expensive, not least because expert evidence is so often required on all three aspects – breach of duty, causation of injury and quantum. It is common for costs to exceed the value of the claim when damages are less than £10,000. A significant proportion of these costs are incurred before it is possible to predict with any accuracy whether or not the claimant has reasonable prospects of success. If initial investigation suggests there are no grounds for further pursuit, the expenditure, for both claimant and defendant, has all been in vain.

If the claimant pursues litigation beyond issue of proceedings they risk having to pay not only their own costs but also the expenses of the defendant who may recover their legal costs from an unsuccessful claimant. Few privately funding claimants are prepared to, or can afford to, take such a risk.

Legal aid

Public funding was introduced in 1949 to assist those otherwise unable to afford legal advice or representation. Criticisms were made of the resulting Legal Aid system: rapidly growing costs with lack of satisfactory control; inability to target resources on priority areas and poor value for money.[10] To weed out cases unlikely to succeed or where costs are disproportionate to value, 'Legal Aid' funding is now only available for clinical negligence claims handled by solicitors holding a clinical negligence franchise, as awarded and monitored by the Legal Services Commission (LSC).

Eligibility criteria for financial assistance from the LSC are stringent. Such assistance is means tested and those with some resources are required to contribute on a regular basis as the claim evolves. Children can obtain assistance in their own name without reference to the resources of their parents and claims made on behalf of children are, therefore, typically publicly funded.

The general rule is that a successful party may recover its costs from its losing opponent. Where claimants are assisted by the LSC, however, in practice the defendant (NHS or medical defence organisation) has to bear its own costs win or lose. This puts the publicly-funded claimant in a very strong financial position since the defendant is bound to suffer financially – by paying both sides' costs if the defence fails or at least his own costs if successful. This creates a powerful incentive to settle such claims before additional legal costs are incurred. Defendants, such as the NHS Litigation Authority may, and do, therefore make representations to the LSC if it is perceived that public funding for a claim is inappropriate, or if the claim is being handled in a way that is wasteful of public funds. The grant of financial assistance by the LSC is subject to review as the case proceeds and may be withdrawn unless the LSC is satisfied that further pursuit is merited and likely to be cost-effective.

Conditional Fee Agreements

A Conditional Fee Agreement (CFA) is a contract between lawyers and claimant which provides for the lawyers' fees to be paid only if the case succeeds in recovering damages. A percentage uplift ('success fee') may be charged in successful cases, to offset the fact that the legal team will remain unpaid in unsuccessful cases. This aspect of CFAs is controversial because of the perceived risk that the claimant's legal team may be inappropriately influenced by having a direct financial interest in achieving a successful outcome.

Funding the defence of clinical negligence claims

When the NHS was established, doctors, unlike other clinical/professional staff, retained responsibility for the costs of claims arising out of clinical care. The escalating volume and value of such claims during the 1980s led to a rapid rise in premiums for professional indemnity, a problem resolved for practitioners employed within NHS hospitals by the advent of NHS indemnity in 1990.[11] However, this applies only for claims arising from events occurring within the course of the Practitioner's NHS employment.

The role of the **medical defence organisations** has changed as a result. While continuing to provide support and assistance to their members, they no longer have financial responsibility for actions relating to NHS hospital care (which are now against trusts rather than individual clinicians), and have no control over the conduct of the litigation. At present, they retain both control and financial responsibility for actions arising from private practice and those brought against General Practitioners and overseas members.

The **Clinical Negligence Scheme for Trusts** (CNST) was introduced in 1995 to pool the cost of claims against NHS trusts. Other than the annual CNST premium, trusts no longer need to set aside funds for clinical litigation. Premiums are set according to the nature and volume of clinical work and the individual trust's claims record. A discount on the premium may be awarded to reflect the performance of each trust's clinical risk management arrangements as judged against the CNST standards.[12]

The National Health Service Litigation Authority (NHSLA) is responsible for handling clinical negligence and personal injury claims against NHS trusts, and for the administration and supervision of the CNST. The Authority also has a remit to sustain or improve patient care, to ensure that patients have access to appropriate remedies and recompense, and that claims handling is carried out consistently and cost-effectively.[13] Centralised management of claims facilitates the compilation of data for the number, nature and cost of clinical claims nationally. It is anticipated in the *NHS Redress Bill* that the NHSLA will have responsibility for management of the proposed Redress Scheme.

Suggested further reading

National Audit Office (NAO). *Handling Clinical Negligence Claims in England: HC 403 session 2000–2001*, HMSO, 2001
(http://www.nao.org.uk/publications/nao_reports/00-01/0001403.pdf)

Making Amends. June 2003. Although some of his recommendations seem unlikely to be implemented, the Chief Medical Officer's report provides useful information on the present system for compensating victims of medical negligence and outlines proposals for reform
www.doh.gov.uk/makingamends/pdf/cmomakingamends.pdf

Localio A *et al*. Results of the Harvard Medical Practice Study III – relation between malpractice claims and adverse events due to negligence. *N Engl J Med* 1991; **325**: 245–251. Seminal study of 30,000 sets of medical records, assessing the incidence of error in care of hospitalised patients (1%) and proportion of those avoidably injured patients who pursue legal claims (2%)

NHS Indemnity – Arrangements for Clinical Negligence Claims in the NHS
http://www.nhsla.com/Publications/ (under 'Claims Publications') – background and details of responsibility for claims since April 1990

Capstick B. The future of clinical negligence litigation? *BMJ* 2004; **328**:457–459 – Brian Capstick comments on the proposed Redress Scheme

References

1. Vincent C, Youngman N. Why do people sue doctors? A study of patients and relatives taking legal action. *Lancet* 1994; **343**: 1609
   Claimants reported that they were pursuing legal action out of a variety of motives. It seems that they were pursuing objectives that litigation could not achieve since the only remedy available was monetary compensation. In 'Making Amends', the CMO proposed that there should be a wider range of possible remedies available.

2. National Audit Office (NAO). *Handling Clinical Negligence Claims in England: HC 403 session 2000–2001*, HMSO, 2001
   (http://www.nao.org.uk/publications/nao_reports/00-01/0001403.pdf)
   Comprehensive study of the cost of clinical negligence claims against the NHS.

3. *Kralj v McGrath [1986] 1 All ER 54*

   Attempted cephalic version of a second twin without general anaesthesia. Aggravated damages deemed wholly inappropriate in action brought in negligence and breach of contract.

4. *Appleton and Others v Garrett [1997] 8 Med LR 75*

   Dentist carried out unnecessary treatment for personal financial gain. Award for the tort of trespass to the person included aggravated damages assessed at 15% of the figure for general damages.

5. *Ruff v The Royal Victoria Infirmary and Associated Hospitals NHS Trust [2001] Lloyd's Rep Med 530*

   Severe cerebral damage following a hypoxic incident in infancy. Negligence was admitted and general damages, some special damages, and the multiplicand for future losses were all agreed. Trial solely on life expectancy and how it should be determined. A clinical rather than statistical approach was preferred.

6. The right of civil partners to bring a claim, as a 'dependant', under the *Fatal Accidents Act, 1976* was created by the *Civil Partnership Act, 2004* (s.83)

7. *Law Reform (Personal Injuries) Act, 1948* s2(4)

   In calculating medical expenses in a damages award, the possibility of using NHS facilities is to be disregarded.

8. In *Making Amends* 2003

   (see 'Suggested further reading') the Chief Medical Officer proposed that claimants should no longer be entitled to recover the costs of private medical treatment, when such services are available on the NHS. This proposal has not been included in the *NHS Redress Bill, 2005* but is apparently still under consideration by the Department of Constitutional Affairs. See also *Parkhouse v North Devon Healthcare Trust [2002] Lloyd's Rep Med 100*. Damages for severely disabled child were discounted to allow for equipment provided by State services.

9. Department of Health. *NHS Redress Bill – Full Regulatory Impact Assessment*, 2005; p13 – DH website (www.doh.gov.uk)

10. 'Report to the Lord Chancellor' on legal aid funding by Sir Peter Middleton 1997 Ch3; www.dca.gov.uk (under reports and reviews)

11. *Claims of medical negligence against NHS hospital and community doctors and dentists*. Department of Health Circular: HC 89(34)

    Health Circular published in 1989 setting out arrangements for NHS indemnity to apply from 1 January 1990. Authorities could no longer require staff to subscribe to a recognised professional defence organisation but should encourage staff to ensure they have 'adequate defence cover as appropriate'. For the first time, the NHS had direct financial responsibility for claims relating to medical treatment and a corresponding interest in reducing error – leading to systems of 'clinical governance'.

12. The CNST Risk Management Standards may be found on the NHSLA website at http://www.nhsla.com/RiskManagement/CnstStandards/

13. *The National Health Service Litigation Authority Framework Document*. Department of Health, September 1996

    Sets out aims, objectives and functions of the NHSLA and how it relates to ministers and the NHS Executive.

5

Legal procedure; dispute resolution; role of expert witnesses

New civil procedure rules came into force in April 1999.[1] They introduced radical reform intended to achieve justice expeditiously, with proportionality between the cost and value of claims. Formal litigation is intended to be a measure of last resort but, once it has begun, the courts have powers to control the conduct of claims and to promote the resolution of disputes without the need for trial.

Parties to the action

Adult patients of sound mind may take legal action in their own name. Actions on behalf of children (below 18 years) and those without the necessary mental capacity are brought in their name by a court-approved 'litigation friend', such as a parent. Actions arising from the death of a patient are brought by the Executor or Administrator and may encompass a claim for damages on behalf of the estate of the deceased as well as a claim for financial support for the deceased's dependants.

In claims relating to the actions of NHS employees, the employing authority has vicarious liability and is named as defendant, whereas in the independent sector and primary care it is typically the individual doctor who is the named defendant (see Chapter 2). Claims brought against more than one defendant raise potential conflict between them and occasionally a defendant may seek to transfer responsibility for an adverse outcome to a third party. The undesirability of legal action between healthcare providers (hospitals or GPs), each blaming the other for causing harm to the patient, is recognised. Accordingly arrangements now exist for such disputes to be resolved avoiding the need for formal legal action whenever possible.[2]

Limitation

The law requires that claims must be commenced within a specified period of the events in question. The *Limitation Act, 1980* sets out the time periods for different types of claim and requires that actions for personal injury must be started either: (i) within 3 years from the date of accrual of the cause of action (*i.e.* the negligent event) or (ii) within 3 years of the date of knowledge (see below).

Date of knowledge is defined as the date on which the claimant first knew or should reasonably have known: (i) the identity of the defendant; **and** (ii) that the injury was significant; **and** (iii) was attributable, in whole or in part, to the act or omission alleged to be negligent.

In effect, therefore, most claims relating to adult patients must commence within 3 years of the events in question, although this period may be longer if, for example, there was a delay in diagnosing cancer about which the patient did not know.

The 3-year period, however, does not operate against children below 18 years of age or persons 'under a disability' (*i.e.* of unsound mind). A person is of unsound mind if, by reason of a mental disorder within the meaning of the *Mental Health Act, 1983,* he is incapable of managing and administering his own affairs. Those of unsound mind either at the time of the incident or as a result of it, are not subject to limitation unless they recover their faculties.

The 3-year period begins to run against a youthful claimant when he reaches 18 years of age. Claims relating to events at birth may, therefore, be made at least up to 21 years after the events in question, or later if the claimant remains under a disability. Claims arising from death must generally be brought within 3 years of the date of the patient's death.

The Limitation Act also provides a discretionary power to the court to allow an action to continue even though it is out of time. Trial of limitation as a preliminary point may then be needed either before, or at the start of, the Trial of the substantive action.

Clinical negligence pre-action protocol

A prescribed pre-action procedure is established for claims alleging clinical negligence. Its purpose is to resolve as many disputes as possible without formal litigation and to assist in the early identification of points of agreement and contention. It is intended that these objectives should be met by the early investigation and appraisal of merit, and reciprocal exchange of expert evidence and conclusions.

The clinical negligence pre-action protocol consists of three essential steps: (i) disclosure of medical records; (ii) Letter of Claim; and (iii) response to the Letter of Claim.

In practice, some latitude on the timing of the steps set out in the pre-action protocol is expected between reasonable litigators but delay carries the potential for cost sanctions imposed by the court.

Disclosure of medical records

A request for access to records may alert the trust or practitioner that a claim is anticipated. Under the pre-action protocol, potential defendants should also be notified of the area of treatment to which the anticipated claim relates. Use of a standard request form is recommended and, in practice, it is usual for the entire records file to be requested. Copy records should be provided within 40 days of the request, and disclosure should be voluntary – it can in any case be enforced by the courts or sought by the patient under the *Data Protection Act, 1998.*

Letter of Claim

This letter is usually based upon initial expert opinion based on the medical notes. Typically prepared by the claimant's legal advisers, it sets out the basis for the claim in formal but non-legalistic terms. It should include:

➢ A summary of the facts, with a chronology if appropriate.

➢ The allegations of breach of duty.

➢ The harm which is alleged to have been caused as a result.

➢ An indication of the value of the claim.

The claimant (*i.e.* his legal advisers) may elect to disclose expert evidence at this stage and is expected to do so if combining the Letter of Claim with an Offer to settle.

A Letter of Claim is not deemed to be legally binding and, if the matter proceeds to litigation, subsequent allegations may differ. Similarly, the assessment of financial loss may be no more than preliminary, particularly in complex or high-value claims.

Response to the Letter of Claim

The Letter of Response should follow within 3 months from the date of the Letter of Claim and should set out:

➢ What, if any, part of the claim is admitted.

➢ What allegations are denied.

➢ Reasoned argument for the denial.

➢ Factual commentary or chronology if the claimant's version is disputed.

The defendant should respond to any Offer to settle, giving reasons for the stance adopted. A Counter-Offer can be made. Evidence refuting liability may also be disclosed – for example, opinion, protocols or guidelines to rebut allegations of breach of duty, or expert evidence to deny causation of injury.

Resolution without legal proceedings

The steps outlined above suffice to induce abandonment of a significant proportion of claims where they are shown to be ill-founded. In others, where the claim is strong, settlement may be negotiated.[3]

Legal proceedings

The formal start of litigation is the 'issue' of Proceedings. A Claim Form (formerly called a Writ or Summons) is submitted to the court, with the requisite fee, and the claim is then registered and allocated a case number. Thereafter, the matter falls under the authority of the court, which may impose control over, and a timetable for, the steps that follow. The Claim Form must be 'served' (*i.e.* delivered by a legally acceptable route) on the defendant or his legal representative (*e.g.* hospital legal department or solicitors) within 4 months of issue. Failure to serve Proceedings by an accepted method and in good time is fatal to a claim and has led to many negligence claims against claimant solicitors.

The Particulars of Claim set out the factual basis for the claim, the allegations of breach of duty and of consequent injury. A medical report substantiating the injury and its consequences ('condition and prognosis report') should be served at the same time as the Particulars, together with a schedule of the special damages claimed (see Chapter 4). The Claim Form, Particulars and report should each incorporate a Statement of Truth. This is a declaration that the party submitting the document believes the facts stated in it are true; a false declaration, made without honest belief in its truth, amounts to contempt of court. Although the claimant's solicitor often makes the declaration on both Claim Form and Particulars, the attestation is to the claimant's belief in the factual veracity of the document and the purpose of this requirement is to prevent spurious or exaggerated claims.

Defending a claim

It is incumbent upon a defendant to file an admission, prepare and serve a Defence, or file an Acknowledgement of service within 14 days of service of the Particulars of Claim. Failure to do so may lead to Judgement against the defendant. Provided service has been acknowledged within 14 days, the defendant has up to 28 days from service of the Particulars of Claim in which to serve the Defence. The parties can agree for this period to be extended for up to another 28 days.

The Defence must state which facts and allegations are admitted, denied or not admitted (*i.e.* require to be proved). Allegations not specifically answered in one of these three ways are deemed to be admitted. The Defence too must include a Statement of Truth by or on behalf of the practitioner or trust.

Subsequent conduct

Once the Defence has been filed (*i.e.* received by the court), further legal exchanges may then follow between the parties – such as a request for further information (further and better particulars) or answers to specific questions (interrogatories).

The parties are then required to co-operate with the court to ensure proper allocation to the appropriate legal 'track'. There are small claims, fast and multitrack options, each with its own arrangements for staging and timing. Clinical negligence claims are usually allocated to the multitrack option, which is reserved for matters considered complex. Thereafter, the court sets a timetable for disclosure of documents, the exchange of witness statements (*i.e.* from witnesses of fact – the claimant/patient and relevant clinical staff), exchange of expert reports and, if necessary, a date for Trial.

Few clinical negligence claims reach trial. Most are either settled by negotiation or discontinued by the claimant.[3] Either party may make an Offer ('Part 36 Offer') to settle on specific terms. Significant cost penalties are incurred if such an Offer is refused and the refusing party subsequently does less well at Trial; a provision which provides a powerful incentive to make or accept carefully considered and targeted proposals.

A number of cases are settled without a formal admission of liability. This may be because economic factors must be taken into consideration by defendants, particularly when the value of the claim is low by comparison with the costs of continuing legal action. It is also relevant that whether successful or unsuccessful, the litigation process can have a profoundly damaging effect on clinical staff involved and the 'costs' of continuing litigation are, therefore, not only financial.[4]

There are obvious potential conflicts between competing requirements to conserve scarce financial resources and preserve the professional reputations of hospitals and practitioners, by presenting a robust defence to claims when appropriate, while at the same time ensuring that those wronged by clinical error are properly compensated. Claims in clinical negligence should not be perceived as an easy route to securing compensation, nor should practitioners feel that justice – or their reputation – are being sacrificed to economic expediency. A better view is to recognise that Legal Aid is rarely continued for cases which do not have at least an arguable chance of succeeding and that liability is often a matter of corporate rather than individual responsibility; in other words, a system error.[5]

'Without prejudice' correspondence

Settlement of disputes, without the need for Trial, is encouraged by the courts and the parties are, therefore, enabled to negotiate without prejudicing their position should Trial ultimately prove necessary. Correspondence intended to achieve settlement is accordingly classified as 'without prejudice' and kept confidential from the court. In practice, it is common to see the 'without prejudice' heading used inappropriately. It should not be confused with legal privilege (see Chapter 6) and if, in fact, the correspondence is not intended to further settlement, the 'without prejudice' heading has no effect.

Alternative dispute resolution (ADR)

This is a generic term encompassing methods other than litigation for resolving disputes.

Arbitration involves an agreed arbitrator determining issues of dispute. The conduct of the arbitration is adversarial in a manner similar to Trial. It is used most often in commercial disputes arising from contract and is rarely used in clinical claims.

Mediation is also rarely used but may be useful where the parties are willing to compromise but need some assistance. The mediator is usually sent documents outlining the parties' positions and then, with their agreement, convenes a meeting attended by both parties and their solicitors. At the meeting, the mediator then enters discussions with each party in turn, typically in separate rooms, exploring the essential elements of, and barriers to, settlement. Knowledge acquired by the mediator is confidential unless permission is given to relay it to the other side. Unlike a litigated settlement, mediation can encompass elements of redress other than financial compensation (*e.g.* an apology, explanation, and commitment to a particular course of action by the defendant). The role of the mediator is to assist the parties to reach an agreed settlement and solutions cannot be imposed.

In practice, such formal methods of ADR are often rendered unnecessary because an outcome, either abandonment or negotiated settlement, may be achieved at less cost through the steps required by the pre-action protocol and court managed litigation. In particular, it is more common to see the resolution of clinical negligence disputes through the exchange of expert reports, and meetings of experts and/or lawyers.

The role of the expert witness

Professional opinion provides the basis for judicial determination of both breach of duty and causation of injury in clinical negligence cases and the courts have power to limit the number of experts, specify their specialism, or direct that evidence on an issue be given by a single expert. A just, legal outcome requires that expert opinion should be accurate, up-to-date, comprehensive, objective and non-partisan. Such ideals have not always been realised and the role of experts in both civil and criminal cases has been highly contentious. Part 35 of the Civil Procedural Rules defines the duties of experts, specifies the content and format of expert reports and requires that they are addressed to the court. The essential duty of the expert is to assist the court and this over-rides any obligation to the party providing instructions or paying the expert's fees.

An expert report must include:

- details of the expert's qualifications
- details of learned literature on which he has relied in formulating his opinion
- the substance of all material instructions provided to him
- clarification of which facts are within the expert's own knowledge
- a summary of the range of medical opinion and reasons for the opinion held
- a summary of the conclusions reached, with any necessary qualification
- a statement confirming that the expert understands his duty to the court, and that he has complied and will continue to comply with this duty.

The report must also be verified by a Statement of Truth confirming the opinion as true and complete, and that facts within the expert's knowledge are identified and believed to be true. Evidence from an expert who flagrantly fails to follow these rules may be disbarred.[6]

Written questions to experts are permitted and the court usually requires that there be a meeting of opposing experts, following which they are expected to prepare a joint statement setting out any matters on which they agree, those on which they disagree and why. Lawyers are not normally present. The introduction of experts' meetings was contentious, as it was feared that it would give doctors the opportunity effectively to decide cases 'behind closed doors'. The safeguard is, however, that throughout their involvement, the experts' primary duty is to the court and the rationale behind any conclusions they reach may be challenged. Assisted by an appropriate agenda agreed between the parties, such meetings can be very effective in narrowing down and clarifying any areas of dispute so that settlement or abandonment may be achieved, or unnecessary time and costs at trial avoided.[7,8] In cases that go to trial, providing the expert gives his evidence to the court honestly and in good faith, he is immune from action by a disgruntled client or others who might be upset by his evidence, either by way of a civil action or professional disciplinary proceedings.[9]

Suggested further reading

Professor Meadow – misconduct and the right to legal immunity – case commentary by David Pannick QC, *The Times* 14 March 2006

Vincent C, Young M. Why do people sue doctors? A study of patients and relatives taking legal action. *Lancet* 1994; **343**: 1609

Pre-action Protocol for Resolution of Clinical Disputes
www.dca.gov.uk/civil/procrules_fin/contents/protocols/prot_rcd.htm

Bark P *et al*. Impact of litigation on senior clinicians: implications for risk management. *Quality Health Care* 1997; **6**: 7–13

Ennis M, Vincent C. The effects of medical accidents and litigation on doctors and patients. *Law Policy* 1994; 16

Vincent C *et al*. The impact of litigation on obstetricians and gynaecologists' *J Obstet Gynaecol* 1994; **14**: 381–387

References

1. The new civil procedure rules followed the review of the civil justice system in England and Wales by Lord Woolf (Access to Justice. HMSO, July 1996)

    Lord Woolf singled-out actions in medical negligence as the area where civil justice failed most conspicuously. He identified disproportion between costs and damages, particularly in low-value cases, a low rate of success, excessive delay, prolonged unwarranted pursuit of unmeritorious claims or indefensible defences, and more intense suspicion and lack of co-operation between the parties than in many other areas of litigation. A damning commentary!

2. NHSLA Circular 98/C1 (*Interparty disputes – litigation between health service bodies*) specifies that 'in no circumstance should any NHS body either issue proceedings or contribution notices against another NHS body, or encourage plaintiffs to do so'.

3. NHS Redress Bill 2005 – Full Regulatory Impact Assessment 2005; p4 at www.dh.gov.uk

   60–70% of clinical negligence claims do not proceed beyond initial contact with a solicitor or disclosure of medical records; 30% of claims formally pursued are abandoned by the claimant; 95% of settlements are reached out of court.

4. Bark P. Effective handling of complaints concerning children. *Curr Paediatr* 1997; **7**: 53–56

   15% of paediatricians had considered giving up medicine because of the threat or actuality of litigation.

5. Reason J. Human error: models and management. *BMJ* 2000; **320**: 768–770

   Psychologist's account of the sources of human error – the person approach and the system approach.

6. *Stevens v Gullis & Anor [1999] EWCA Civ 1978*

   In a building dispute, an 'expert' in building surveying demonstrated disregard for the obligations of the Civil Procedure Rules on experts and the duty to assist the court. The expert was not considered an appropriate person to give expert evidence in court and his participation was excluded. Decision upheld by Court of Appeal.

7. *Hubbard and Ors v Lambeth, Southwark and Lewisham Health Authority and Ors [2002] Lloyd's Rep Med 8*

   Court ordered meeting of experts not precluded by sensitivity of those who had criticised a pre-eminent colleague in written reports, which had already been exchanged.

8. *Peet v Mid-Kent Healthcare NHS Trust [2002] Lloyd's Rep Med 33*

   Court directed joint instruction of non-medical quantum experts; claimant sought to confer with them in the absence of the defendants. Such a meeting was opposed by the defendants and rejected by the court as inconsistent with CPR. The desirability of single quantum experts was reiterated. The report is followed by a useful commentary from three experienced Clinical Negligence Counsel on the practical implications of instructing single experts, particularly in high-value claims.

9. *Meadow v GMC [2006] EWHC 146 Admin* (c.f. *Times Law Report* (22 February 2006) – 'Immunity for honest but mistaken expert witness'

   The justice system requires that witnesses should be willing to give evidence to the court without fear of being sued by a disgruntled client or others who might be upset by the evidence given. In exceptional circumstances, an expert's evidence or conduct might justify referral by the court to a professional disciplinary body but otherwise the expert is protected from such disciplinary action. In this case the complaint to the GMC Fitness to Practice Panel should not have been pursued and appeal against the finding of the Panel was accordingly successful. 'Experts can give evidence free from the fear of subsequent disciplinary action unless they act so contrary to their obligations to their profession and to the court that the court decides to make a complaint. Only in such circumstances will disciplinary action be permissible.' Appeal by GMC to the Court of Appeal pending.

6

Confidentiality and disclosure

Patients must feel free to reveal to their doctors any information necessary for their medical care, even if it is sensitive, intimate or embarrassing, and personal information relating to patients, whether private or NHS, is held under a common law duty of confidentiality. The general rule is that confidential information must not be released to any third party without the consent of the patient. This rule can be waived if disclosure is required by statute (*e.g.* when it concerns notifiable diseases), or where the safety of the public or an identified individual is at risk.[1] Many of the exceptions are a matter of professional discretion rather than of law,[2] the guiding principle being that the practitioner must be able to give good reason for disclosure.

Public concern about the unnecessary or inappropriate recording, retention or dissemination of personal details has led to legislation and recommendations which seek to resolve tension between the rights of individuals to privacy and the needs of society for disclosure of relevant information in some circumstances. This tension is particularly acute in the healthcare setting, where the recording and sharing of intimate personal information is a prerequisite to good clinical practice.

Safeguards should be in place to protect the security and confidentiality of clinical information, whilst allowing for its appropriate use. In 1997, the Caldicott Committee reported variable compliance with good data protection practice and *Health Service Circular 99(012)* sets out the requirements for all trusts to appoint a Caldicott Guardian whose responsibilities include the supervision of local protocols governing the handling of patient-identifiable information and its disclosure across organisational boundaries.

There followed, in 2003, an *NHS Code of Practice on Confidentiality*[3] and, in 2005, the *NHS Care Record Guarantee*[4] set out a series of commitments on how electronic records would be used. Legislation has also defined the rights of patients and corresponding responsibilities of practitioners.

Relevant statutory provisions

The *Access to Health Records Act, 1990* marked a major devepment, introducing a statutory right for patients to see records about them. Although now largely superceded by the Data Protection legislation (below), the Act still affords rights of access to the records of deceased persons to personal representatives and those who may have a claim arising from the patient's death.

The *Data Protection Act, 1998* imposes duties on data controllers and processors and provides patients with rights of access to manual and electronic records, (subject to specific exceptions) and rights of verification and correction.

The *Human Rights Act, 1998* confirms a responsibility to prevent disclosure of information imparted in confidence. Article 8 defines a right to respect for private and family life, home and correspondence which includes a right to privacy but includes exceptions based on public need.

The *Access to Medical Reports Act, 1988* provides a right to patients to inspect or be supplied with a copy of medical reports prepared about them for employment or insurance purposes by a practitioner who is, or has been, responsible for their clinical care. Reports prepared by an independent practitioner who has never adopted a therapeutic relationship with the patient are not covered by either the *Data Protection Act, 1998* or the *Access to Medical Reports Act, 1988*.

The *Freedom of Information Act, 2000* provides for access to non-personal information held by public authorities, for example policies for the provision of services and reports reviewing that provision. Section 40 of the Act requires that personal data are largely exempt from the freedom of information provisions, and are handled in accordance with the Data Protection Act.

The *Health and Social Care Act, 2001* permits the Secretary of State for Health to regulate the processing of patient information if required in the public interest or in the interests of improving patient care. Subordinate legislation, the *Health Service (Control of Patient Information) Regulations, 2002*, accordingly makes provision for disclosure of confidential information without patient consent for the purposes of public health surveillance, research, audit and the maintenance of cancer registries.[5]

Under the *Public Health (Control of Disease) Act, 1984* and the *Public Health (Infectious Diseases) Regulations, 1988*, a doctor whose patient has a notifiable disease, such as cholera, yellow fever, small pox or typhus, is obliged to inform the local authority. Other statutory provisions which require the disclosure of information include Section 19 of the *Terrorism Act, 2000*; and *The Abortion Regulations, 1991*.

Disclosure of medical records

Health records are defined in the *Data Protection Act, 1998* as any record which consists of: (i) information relating to the physical or mental health or condition of an individual; and (ii) has been made by, or on behalf of, a health professional in connection with the care of that individual.

The term 'any record' includes paper-based records, and information held electronically in the form of microfiche, optical disks, X-ray films, videotapes, compact disks, photographs or photographic slides.

Care, as defined in the *Access to Medical Reports Act, 1988*, includes examination, investigation or diagnosis for the purposes of any form of medical treatment. Documentation which does not lie within these definitions, such as incident reports or complaints correspondence, should be filed separately to lessen the risk of unauthorised disclosure if there is a request for 'the medical notes'.

There are a number of exceptions to the right of individuals to access records under the Data Protection Act and Access to Health Records Act, most importantly if:

➢   A health professional believes disclosure is likely to cause serious harm to the physical or mental health of the patient or any other person.

➢   The information relates to, or has been provided by, an identifiable third party who has not consented to disclosure.

➢   In the context of deceased persons, there is written evidence that disclosure would be contrary to the wishes of the deceased.

These exemptions might, for example, apply in relation to mentally vulnerable patients, or where a diagnosis or test result has been documented but not yet communicated to the patient. In practice, however, it is relatively rare for these exemptions to apply and, in the absence of good reason to the contrary, disclosure is to be expected.

Disclosure in the context of litigation

Voluntary disclosure of case notes to a patient's solicitor requires the consent of the patient or Litigation Friend. The claimant's express authority is not required for disclosure to the trust or practitioner's legal advisers when a patient intimates an intention to take action against them. Confidentiality in this circumstance is either deemed to have been waived or it can be argued that disclosure is required in the public interest to ensure efficient and just disposal of the case.

Compulsory disclosure can be enforced by court order against a potential defendant before an action begins, or against an uninvolved third party after proceedings have commenced. Disclosure of medical and nursing notes is now usually made voluntarily and most disputes centre on the release of records of patients with mental illness.[6] Whilst a patient pursuing legal action may refuse to consent to disclosure of their medical records to a defendant, if the records are likely to be relevant and justice requires the defendant to have access to them, the court may prevent continuance of the claim until consent is given to their disclosure.

Claims for compensation arising from alleged breach of confidentiality[7] are rare because such a claim can only succeed if:

➢   The information has the necessary quality of confidence (*e.g.* is not public knowledge).

➢   The information is imparted in circumstances such that the person receiving information must have known, or is held to have agreed, that it was confidential.

➢   Unauthorised use of the information has caused detriment to the party imparting it.

The *Data Protection Act, 1998* makes statutory provision for compensation if a data processor contravenes the terms of the Act but here too the claimant must prove that damage resulted.

Breach of confidentiality in the public interest

In exceptional circumstances, breach of confidentiality may be justified to protect the public, for example, where a patient continues to drive against medical advice. Disclosure may also be justified to assist in the prevention or detection of serious crime, for example, where a mentally ill patient has expressed violent intentions towards an identified individual. Indeed, failure to pro-actively disclose this information may be negligent.[8] Disclosure of information should, however, be proportionate and to an appropriate authority.[9]

The *Road Traffic Act, 1988* gives powers to the police to require the provision of information to identify a driver alleged to have committed a traffic offence.[10] In other cases, pursuant to the *Police and Criminal Evidence Act, 1984*, the police may ask the court to issue a warrant to search for 'excluded material', including medical records. In cases of doubt over the 'public interest' of disclosing confidential information, the doctor's position is protected by refusing voluntary disclosure and asking the police to obtain such a warrant.

Legal professional privilege

Individuals and organisations (*e.g.* trusts) are entitled to correspond confidentially with their lawyers. Thus documents prepared for use in actual or contemplated litigation or to obtain legal advice from a qualified lawyer are 'privileged' and protected from disclosure.[11] However, litigation or legal advice as the sole or prime purpose at the time of preparation is the cardinal requirement and the class of documents protected from disclosure is, therefore, restricted.[12] Thus incident reports prepared for clinical governance purposes, or internal correspondence arising under the Complaints Procedure, will be prone to disclosure.[13] It is accordingly advisable that information recorded in anticipation of litigation or to obtain legal advice should be documented separately from information that is recorded for other purposes.

The results of research and audit can be published or disclosed without breach of confidentiality provided individual patients cannot be identified.[14,15] Disclosure of medical records to a public body can also be ordered if there is a sufficiently compelling public interest to do so and provided there are sufficient and adequate safeguards.[16]

Disclosure of medical records after death

The duty to respect a patient's confidence will ordinarily persist after the patient's death.[17] The *Access to Health Records Act, 1990*, however, provides for disclosure of records to a deceased's personal representative or any person who may have a claim arising from the patient's death. It is doubtful if the coroner has a power to secure disclosure of notes before an Inquest. However, he is required to examine, on Oath, all persons having knowledge as to the facts of the death whom he considers it expedient to examine, can issue a subpoena requiring attendance (with penalties for non-compliance) and can impose a fine upon a witness who, without lawful excuse, refuses to answer a question put to him. In view of these provisions, it is hardly surprising that disclosure of notes to both coroner and family is usually given on request.

Is there a duty of *post-facto* candour?

There is no direct judicial authority for a legal duty to inform a patient if their care has been affected by an adverse event/incident. The concept is, however, widely and increasingly endorsed and the GMC, in *Good Medical Practice* (para 17) advises that, if a patient suffers serious harm, a full explanation should be provided to the patient. The National Patient Safety Agency also advocates post-incident openness.[18]

A finding of negligence is not inevitable if a report advocating system change after an adverse incident is disclosed. Negligence is determined by the standards which pertained at the time of the incident: being wise after the event is not necessarily indicative of poor practice. There are, however, arguments to suggest that such reports should be exempt from disclosure, to facilitate an uninhibited incident reporting system and learning from adverse outcomes[19] without fear of adverse consequences.

Loss or destruction of records (including X-rays and charts) is likely to be interpreted to the disadvantage of the record-holder, even if wholly innocent. This is particularly so if records are destroyed when it is already clear that legal proceedings are in contemplation.[20]

Suggested further reading

GMC Guidance. *Confidentiality: Protecting and providing information*. 2004 – updated guidance available at http://www.gmc-uk.org/guidance/library/ confidentiality.asp covers general and specific issues and has a Frequently Asked Questions section

NHS Code of Practice on Confidentiality (November 2003) – a detailed document providing practical guidance and endorsed by the Information Commissioner, GMC and BMA. Available in the Policy and Guidance section of the DH website (www.dh.gov.uk)

www.informationcommissioner.gov.uk – website for the Information Commissioner, providing guidance and information on the Data Protection and Freedom of Information Acts, and details of adjudication decisions made by the Commissioner

NHS Records Management – Code of Practice. April 2006 – extensive guidance on record creation, keeping and disposal including 40 pages on legal and professional obligations (www.dh.gov.uk)

Health Service Circular HSC 1998/153. *Using electronic patient records in hospital: legal requirements and good practice* available at the Publications and Statistics section of the DH website at www.dh.gov.uk

Department for Constitutional Affairs. *Public sector data sharing – guidance on the law*. November 2003, available at http://www.dca.gov.uk/foi/sharing/

Guidelines on disclosure of information in relation to gunshot wounds, agreed between the GMC and Association of Chief Police Officers and supported by British Association for Accident and Emergency Medicine; available at www.gmc-uk.org/guidance/library/reporting_gunshot_wounds.asp

References

1. *W v Egdell [1989] 2 WLR 689*
    Psychiatrist voluntarily disclosed to a mental hospital and the Home Office an unfavourable report on a paranoid schizophrenic, who had been convicted of manslaughter but was, by then, seeking less stringent detention. Public interest in disclosure outweighed W's private interests.

2. GMC. *Confidentiality: Protecting and Providing Information*. Guidelines provided by the GMC, 2004
    Amplifies the GMC's general guidance in *Good Medical Practice*, including when information may be disclosed without consent. Available at http://www.gmc-uk.org/guidance/library/confidentiality.asp

3. *NHS Code of Practice on Confidentiality*. 2003
    Available in the Policy and Guidance section of the DH website (www.dh.gov.uk).

4. *NHS The Care Record Guarantee*. May 2005. www.connectingforhealth.nhs.uk/crdb/
    A series of commitments on how nationally held electronic records will be used.

5. A register of applications approved by the Secretary of State, enabling release of otherwise confidential information, is available at http://www.advisorybodies.doh.gov.uk/piag/
    The register lists diverse studies and geographically wide-ranging audits, evidencing the beneficial use to which information may be put and the need to balance this against data protection considerations.

6. *R v Mid-Glamorgan FHSA ex parte Martin [1994] 5 Med LR 383*
    Schizophrenic patient sought disclosure of medical records antedating Access to Health Records Act. Court of Appeal held there was no common law right of access and claimant was excluded by the terms of the Act.

7. *Cornelius v de Taranto [2001] EWCA Civ 1511*
    Forensic psychiatrist, concerned about the mental health of the claimant, sent a copy of a medicolegal report arising in the context of alleged unfair dismissal to the claimant's GP and a consultant psychiatrist without consent.

The report was treated as part of the claimant's NHS 'medical records'. The claimant was awarded £3,000 for breach of confidentiality.

8. 'Sister who saw killing wins record trauma sum', *The Times*, 5 November 2001
    When a dangerously ill psychiatric patient was released to go home, he killed his mother and then himself. The Trust accepted it had a duty of care to the patient's family, and admitted liability for the post-traumatic stress disorder caused to the patient's sister who witnessed the deaths. In the US case of *Tarasoff v Regents of University of California (1976) 17 Cal 3d 425*, it was held that a psychologist owed a duty of care to a particular woman, murdered by one of his patients who had expressed an intention to kill her. She should have been forewarned, even though this would have breached confidentiality.

9. *Duncan v Medical Practitioners' Disciplinary Committee (1986) 1 NZLR 513 (New Zealand)*
    A GP who was concerned that a bus driver was unfit to drive was entitled to notify the responsible authority. It was not appropriate for him also to warn the driver's potential passengers.

10. *Hunter v Mann (1974) 2WLR 742*
    A police officer, acting under the then *Road Traffic Act, 1972*, asked the defendant doctor for information which would identify the driver of a stolen car who was suspected of dangerous driving. The doctor refused to breach confidentiality and was convicted of a statutory offence.

11. *Three Rivers District Council v Bank of England (No 6) [2004] UKHL 48*
    An attempt was made to obtain access to correspondence and documents prepared by or for the Bank of England and its lawyers in preparation for the inquiry into the role of the Bank in the collapse of BCCI. The House of Lords held that communication with a lawyer, acting in his role as legal adviser, is protected from disclosure even if it relates to presentation and other matters relating to a regulatory investigation, rather than only to legal advice on the client's rights and obligations. Such protection will equally apply to advice and assistance given by a lawyer in the relevant legal context to his client with reference to inquiries such as coroners' inquests and regulatory investigations (*e.g.* disciplinary matters before the GMC).

12. *Lask v Gloucester HA [1991] 2 Med LR 379*
    A confidential Accident Report was prepared after patient fell in hospital grounds. It considered the possibility of future litigation and measures to prevent repetition of the accident. Disclosure of the accident report was ordered on grounds that the second purpose was at least as important as the first.

13. *Hewlett-Parker v St George's Healthcare NHS Trust [1998] 4 Med Lit 3*
    Claimant's application granted for pre-action discovery of the defendant's complaints file.

14. *R v Department of Health ex parte Source Informatics Ltd [2000] Lloyd's Rep Med 76*
    Court of Appeal decision permitting disclosure of anonymised prescription data. Issue deemed to be of such importance that representation and intervention in the appeal were allowed on behalf of the GMC, MRC, ABPI and the National Pharmaceutical Association.

15. *H (A Healthcare Worker) v Associated Newspapers Ltd (2002) EWCA Civ 195*
    H was an HIV-positive healthcare worker. Publication of his specialty was

permitted, but not his place of work, since it may be a breach of confidentiality to publish information from which an individual may be identified, even though the actual identity is not published.

16. *A Health Authority v X and Ors [2002] Lloyd's Rep Med 139*

Health Authority sought disclosure of patient records to assist investigation of a possible breach of GP Terms of Service. Disclosure to a public body was deemed contrary to the *Human Rights Act, 1998* but can be (and was) authorised if there is a compelling public interest satisfying criteria of necessity and proportionality, and sufficient and adequate safeguards are available. The duty to hold the records in confidence is transferred to the recipients.

17. *Re C (Adult Patient: Publicity) [1996] 2 FLR 251*

An order was granted to prevent identification of a patient in PVS and his family, even after his death.

18. The National Patient Safety Agency (NPSA) 'Being Open' policy

Advises healthcare staff to apologise to patients and families if a mistake or error is made that leads to moderate or severe harm or death. Further details are available at http://www.npsa.nhs.uk/health/resources/beingopen. The provision of appropriate apologies and explanations in the context of an adverse result is also supported by the NHS Litigation Authority (http://www.npsa.nhs.uk/site/media/documents/1340_Endorsements.pdf) which, in February 2002 issued Circular 02/02 'Apologies and Explanations' (available at www.nhsla.com/publications).

19. 'The perils of saying sorry' *Hospital Doctor* 17, November 2005

Jonathan Haslam of the Medical Protection Society comments on the disclosure of incident reports.

20. *Hammond v W Lancs HA [1998] Lloyd's Rep Med 146*

Destruction of X-rays following receipt of a letter before action, because hospital did not consider they were part of a patient's medical records, was regarded by the judge as 'wholly unacceptable'.

7

Consent; minors and the mentally incapacitated; research; training

Any medical procedure, which is invasive or involves touching the patient, is a tort (battery/trespass to the person) unless there is a valid defence. The most obvious defence is consent. If the patient cannot give consent the doctor may rely on a statutory defence (*e.g.* the Mental Health Act) or a common law defence (*e.g.* 'necessity') if available.

In a claim for battery, it is not necessary to prove that 'injury' has occurred – the mere fact of non-consensual touching is sufficient to establish liability. However, actions for battery claiming invalid consent to medical treatment rarely succeed,[1] provided that the claimant has consented in general terms.[2] Allegations that the consent to treatment was invalid because the patient was inadequately informed are, therefore, brought in negligence, not battery. If the claim is to succeed in negligence, it is necessary to prove that the patient, if properly informed, would have withheld consent to treatment at that time.[3] In extreme circumstances, touching without proper consent in the medical context can give rise to criminal liability (see Chapter 10).

The nature of consent

Implied consent is the basis for many diagnostic or therapeutic interventions – agreement is implied by a course of conduct (*e.g.* the removal of clothing to facilitate venepuncture). **Express oral consent** is usually obtained for more substantive contacts such as intimate physical examination. **Express written consent** is preferred for procedures that are more than minimally invasive, require general anaesthesia or are associated with significant risk. There is, however, no difference in law between oral and written consent but a signed consent form is of evidential value in case of subsequent dispute. The fact that a consent form has been signed may not, of itself, prove that the consent was valid (*e.g.* adequately informed) but it is of assistance, particularly if the doctor has documented the risks that he has explained to the patient and that the patient has been given an opportunity to raise any concerns. The revised NHS standard consent forms are designed to provide better evidence than in the past of the information that has been relayed to the patient.

What constitutes valid consent?

Consent to treatment is only valid if the patient is: (i) acting voluntarily; (ii) provided with sufficient information; and (iii) competent to take the decision.

Was consent given voluntarily?

This is rarely a cause of conflict but evidence of overbearing parental pressure to refuse treatment has sufficed to persuade the court to authorise blood transfusion to a former Jehovah's Witness.[4] However, there must be evidence that there was undue influence[5] and that it over-ruled volition.[6]

What constitutes 'sufficient information'?

There are some circumstances in which medical treatment carries risks of such significance that no reasonable doctor should fail to warn their patient of them. It is not, however, deemed necessary to inform patients of every possible side-effect of treatment and sufficiency of information is defined at English law by the *'Bolam'* principle – judicial appraisal, based on professional opinion, of compliance with reasonable medical practice.[7] There is an appropriate desire to avoid causing patients unnecessary concern over risks that are very unlikely to eventuate but current recommendations, based on recent case law, advocate more detailed disclosure than has been customary in the past.[8-10] Factors to consider when determining what constitutes 'appropriate' information should include both the magnitude of the possible adverse consequence and the likelihood that it will occur. The safe approach is to provide that information of which the prudent patient would wish to be aware before deciding whether to agree to treatment.[11] It is also relevant to take into account any particular concerns or features specific to the individual patient. The risk of loss of sight in one eye will, for example, be of particular importance to a patient who already has diminished sight in the other eye. Giving the patient an opportunity to ask questions or raise concerns, and documenting that you have done so, can be a safeguard against complaint in this respect.

Claimants bringing an action in negligence, founded on the allegation that the information given fell below an acceptable standard, must be able to show:

➤ That the information given was, in fact, inadequate by accepted standards **and**

➤ Consent would have been withheld at that time had the proper information been supplied.

It can be difficult for the claimant to satisfy the court on the second limb of the test if the risk that materialised occurs infrequently and worthwhile benefit was anticipated from the treatment.[12] However, such actions may succeed if the claimant can provide convincing testimony that he would have either refused or at least postponed consent had sufficient information been given.[13]

Assessing mental competence and the refusal of consent to medical treatment

Competence to consent to treatment[14] requires the ability to: (i) understand the information given; (ii) retain and believe that information; and (iii) use it to reach a reasoned decision.

Lack of competence may be permanent or transitory and is 'decision-specific' – even patients of limited mental capacity may be competent to consent to some less serious treatment. In the absence of evidence to the contrary, adult patients are presumed to be competent to give consent or refuse consent to treatment. In practice, doctors assess mental competence as a matter of routine in the course of everyday contact with their patients and, at law, their medical qualification is entirely adequate for these purposes. In difficult cases, however, the assessment of competence may require independent psychiatric advice. Where doubt persists, the court may be asked to make a declaration on whether or not the patient is competent.[15]

As a basic principle, where a competent, informed, adult patient acting voluntarily makes it clear that he does not wish to receive treatment it is unlawful to administer that treatment, even if it is objectively in his medical best interests. Even life-saving treatment initiated or continued in contravention of the clearly expressed wishes of a competent patient can found a claim for damages.[16] Such refusal of consent to treatment may be asserted in advance, by means of an 'advance directive' or 'living will' provided that: (i) the decision was made when the patient was competent, properly informed and acting voluntarily; and (ii) the decision covers the circumstances which prevail when treatment is contemplated.[17]

If, during a procedure for which consent has been properly obtained, a patient requests that it be terminated, his wishes should be respected in so far as is possible whilst protecting his welfare (*e.g.* once medical instrumentation has been safely removed).[18] Whilst the principles of autonomy and self-determination enable the patient to refuse treatment, they do not entitle the patient to insist on receiving a particular medical treatment and a patient cannot oblige a doctor to administer a treatment that the doctor considers to be adverse to the patient's clinical need. Insofar as there is an obligation to provide treatment, this arises from the duty of care owed to the patient – not because the patient demands treatment. Where a doctor feels unable to offer a treatment requested by a patient, he should consider referring the patient for a second opinion.

Treatment without consent

The doctrine of necessity is the legal justification for providing treatment to patients who temporarily lack the competence to provide valid consent. The obvious example is that of the patient brought to hospital unconscious. The justification extends, however, only to those measures that are required to avoid imminent danger to the life or health of the patient where delay would be unreasonable.[19] Non-urgent treatment is not justified by necessity and, if performed without consent, may prompt disciplinary proceedings and/or a claim for damages.[20,21] Any treatment should be proportionate to the danger faced by the patient and limited to what is reasonably required in the best interests of the patient in the interim before he recovers competence. 'Necessity' does not justify treating an incompetent patient in a way that he had expressly rejected whilst still competent.

In the case of patients who are permanently incompetent or incapable of communication, the doctrine has broader effect. It renders lawful, despite the absence of consent, such treatment as a reasonable doctor would in the circumstances give, acting in the best interests of the patient.[22]

In very prescribed circumstances, the *Mental Health Act, 1983* allows for patients to be detained and/or treated for mental illness, even against their will.[23] The Act cannot, however, be invoked to justify treatment or procedures unconnected with the mental condition, and for these purposes normal consent principles apply.[24] In even more limited situations, treatment without consent is permitted in the interests of public safety under public health legislation.

Parental responsibility and consent by or on behalf of children and young people

'Parental responsibility' refers to the rights, duties and powers that most parents have in respect of their children and includes the authority to consent to medical treatment of a child, in so far as such treatment is in the child's best interests. Accordingly, those parents or guardians with parental responsibility can give valid consent to treatment for patients up to the age of majority (18 years). It is necessary only to obtain the consent of one parent other than in exceptional circumstances.[25] The *Children Act, 1989* sets out circumstances in which others may consent on behalf of the child, for example when acting *in loco parentis*.[26]

A child's biological (birth) mother automatically has parental responsibility for her child, unless the child has been adopted or was born as a result of gamete donation or surrogacy, in which case the rules under the *Human Fertilisation and Embryology Act 1990* apply. A biological father automatically has parental responsibility if married to the mother at the time of the child's birth, or at some time thereafter, and neither parent loses parental responsibility as a result of divorce. The relevant local authority acquires parental responsibility, shared with the parents, while a child is subject to a Care Order. Where the child has been formally adopted, parental responsibility is transferred to the adoptive parents who become the child's legal parents.

The law relating to parental responsibility for unmarried fathers changed on 1 December 2003. For children born before 1 December 2003 only the mother automatically has parental responsibility. For children born after 1 December 2003, on the other hand, the unmarried father also automatically has parental responsibility, so long as he is named on the child's birth certificate. In any event, unmarried fathers may acquire parental responsibility by marrying the mother, by entering into a parental responsibility agreement with the mother, or through a parental responsibility order made by a court.

Section 8 of the *Family Law Reform Act, 1969* creates a presumption that young people aged 16 and 17 years are able to give valid consent to surgical, medical or dental treatment as if they were an adult. The usual criteria for competence apply (as above) but the presumption does not cover the donation of organs and blood, or participation in research. When a child of this age refuses treatment that refusal may, however, be over-ruled by a person with parental responsibility.[27] The power to over-rule must be exercised only in the best interests of the patient, and the psychological effect of having a decision over-ruled must be considered. Practitioners may consider it appropriate to administer treatment in the face of such refusal only where there is a risk of grave or irreversible physical or mental harm. In exceptional cases, the court may be asked to declare whether treatment without the patient's or parents' consent is in the best interests of the child and, therefore, lawful.[28]

Children below the age of 16 years can give valid consent to medical treatment without parental involvement provided they have sufficient maturity and intelligence fully to understand the implications of what is proposed,[29] a test widely referred to as 'Gillick competence'. A higher level of maturity and understanding is necessary to give consent to more serious procedures and a child under 16 years may, therefore, be competent to consent to some interventions but not others. If competent, they are, however, entitled to the protection of medical confidentiality.[30] Decisions of a Gillick-competent patient to refuse treatment should be given due regard but may be over-ruled, as above.[31]

Particular care must be taken when there is dispute between the parent/guardian and medical staff as to whether or not a particular medical treatment is in a child's best interests.[32] Due regard must be given to the rights of the parents to family autonomy but parents cannot veto treatment that is in the child's best interests or require that inappropriate treatment should be given. If it proves difficult to achieve agreement, practitioners would be well advised to seek a second opinion or request review by a clinical ethics committee, maintaining the involvement of the family as far as possible. If dispute persists, however, an application may be made to the court for a ruling. Whilst the views and wishes of parents/guardians and medical staff will be taken into account by the court, each case is decided on its own merits and it is the court that determines what would be in the child's best interests.[33-35]

Consent on behalf of the mentally incompetent/incapacitated adult

Fundamental principles, relating to the care of patients who do not have the mental competence to make decisions regarding their medical treatment, have been established by caselaw. In large part, these have now been incorporated into the *Mental Capacity Act, 2005* (the text of which can be accessed via www.dca.gov.uk/capacity). The provisions of the Act are not effective until April 2007; in the interim, codes of practice arising from the Act are anticipated. Until then the common law position prevails.

The doctrine of necessity allows treatment to be given to a mentally incompetent adult so long as it is in accordance with reasonable medical practice and is in the patient's best interests.[36] Courtesy and professional propriety require that practitioners should consult with relatives concerning the patient's best interests and to seek any information that may be available concerning what the patient would have wished. Such consultation is of particular importance on sensitive questions such as a decision not to attempt resuscitation or to withhold or withdraw treatment. The views of relatives are not, however, legally binding and, in particularly contentious cases such as sterilisation for contraceptive purposes or difficult cases on the withdrawal of supportive therapy,[37,38] the court may be asked to make a declaration as to the lawfulness or otherwise of proposed treatment of a mentally incompetent adult.

In these circumstances, the court does not 'authorise' treatment that would otherwise be unlawful and will not dictate that treatment must be given;[39] however, it will make a declaration as to whether or not proposed treatment or withdrawal of treatment will be lawful. Treatment without a declaration is, therefore, not necessarily 'unlawful' – it is merely unprotected by the court. Good practice or caution may thus require doctors to seek a declaration where the legality of proposed treatment is in doubt but this is not something they are required to do as a matter of law.[40]

The test adopted by the court in considering such cases is that of best interests, a concept easy to understand but difficult to define. In the context of a proposal to undertake vasectomy on a man with Down's syndrome, it was held to encompass medical, emotional and all other welfare issues pertaining to the incompetent person.[38] No restrictions are, however, placed on the range of factors that the court will take into account.

In the absence of a clearly identifiable and accessible source from which to obtain consent on behalf of mentally incompetent adults, both patients and practitioners have appeared to be vulnerable. Implementation of the Mental Capacity Act will enable competent patients to appoint a proxy to act on their behalf if they should lose capacity in future. A newly established Court of Protection will also be enabled to appoint deputies empowered to take some decisions on behalf of incompetent adults. In the meantime, the key guiding principles remain those of acting in accordance with reasonable medical practice and in the patient's best interests.

Consent for research and teaching

Conflict over research has spawned virtually no English caselaw but professional recommendations require that particular care should be taken to provide the fullest possible information before subjects are recruited to any research project, therapeutic or non-therapeutic. Information should preferably be in writing and approved before use by the appropriate Research Ethics Committee. The Medical Research Council, The Royal College of Physicians and Association of British Pharmaceutical Industries have all offered guidelines and so too have the Medical Defence Organisations. Were a claim to arise from research, it is likely that these professional guidelines would be recognised by the court as defining the appropriate standards of practice.[41]

The Law Commission considered it would be unlawful to undertake non-therapeutic research on adults incompetent to consent[42] although professional opinion increasingly accepts such investigation as ethical provided it is 'not against the interests' of the subject. Similarly, professional opinion accepts that participation of children in non-therapeutic research is not necessarily unethical provided:

➢ Consent has been obtained from one or both parents and a research ethics committee.

➢ The research entails no more than minimal risk.

➢ It does not entail any suffering for the child.

➢ The child does not appear to object.

The use of experimental treatment in children or incompetent adults is to be determined in the patient's best interests.[39]

Gaining clinical experience is a necessary part of medical education and it is inevitable that trainees, before or after graduation, will be involved in clinical procedures. Consent is not invalidated provided no commitment has been given that a named practitioner will undertake the treatment. It is the *procedure* to which consent has been given. However, the UK Department of Health recommends that explicit consent should be obtained for the involvement of students.[43] If some element of the procedure is changed or extended beyond usual practice, merely to permit students to learn or experienced practitioners to maintain their expertise, specific consent should be obtained.

Suggested further reading

Reference guide to consent for examination or treatment. Provides a review of law relating to consent as at 2001 and is available at the DH website (www.dh.gov.uk Policy and Guidance section)

Parental responsibility. Guidance from the BMA Ethics Department, September 2005 http://www.bma.org.uk/ap.nsf/Content/Parental

A summary of the *Mental Capacity Act, 2005* may be found at the Publications and Statistics (Acts and Bills) section of the DH website

Advice on the decision of the European Court of Human Rights in the case of *HL v UK* (the *'Bournewood'* case). Department of Health Interim Guidance, December 2004 http://www.dh.gov.uk/assetRoot/04/09/79/92/04097992.pdf

Practice note (Declaratory proceedings: medical and welfare decisions for adults who lack capacity) sets out cases in which a court declaration should be obtained. Available on the website of the Official Solicitor – www.officialsolicitor.gov.uk

Best practice Guidance for doctors and other health professionals on the Provision of Advice and Treatment to Young People under 16 on Contraception, Sexual and Reproductive Health, 2004. Department of Health (at www.dh.gov.uk) and unsuccessful judicial review challenge at *R v Axon v Secretary of State for Health [2006] EWHC 37 (Admin)*

References

1. *Appleton & Others v Garrett [1997] 8 Med LR 75*
    Unnecessary dental treatment undertaken for financial gain. Negligence was admitted but unusually claimants also succeeded in an action for 'trespass to the person' (which includes battery) and were awarded aggravated damages.

2. *Chatterton v Gerson [1987] 1 All ER 257*
    Neurological damage after a phenol nerve block. Patient deemed to have been informed 'in broad terms' of the nature of the procedure: consent was held to be real and action in battery failed.

3. *Chester v Afshar [2004] UKHL 41*

   Patient developed cauda equina syndrome following spinal surgery. The defendant, in private practice, had failed to warn the patient that the risk carried a 1–2% risk of paraplegia. In a controversial decision, the House of Lords determined that the claimant was entitled to recover damages – it was sufficient for her to prove that she would have postponed her decision and surgery, even if she may ultimately have consented with the same risks. The lack of adequate information was treated by the Lords as an affront to the patient's right to autonomy. Note: the claimant succeeded in factual circumstances not dissimilar to those of *Sidaway [1985]* below,[7] in which case the claimant failed. The approach of the court to these claims has changed in the interim.

4. *Re T (Adult: refusal of treatment) [1992] 3 Med LR 306*

   Court of Appeal decision confirming the right of competent adults to refuse life-saving treatment and establishing criteria for validity of such a decision. See also *Re MB [1997] 8 Med LR 217* – mother had a right to refuse caesarean section even if it meant the death of her unborn child. The fetus had no rights at law such that the mother could be compelled to undergo surgery against her wishes.

5. *Poynter v Hillingdon HA BMJ 1997 314:1224*

   Unsuccessful claim for damages on behalf of child severely brain damaged after pioneering cardiac transplant. Parents alleged inadequate information was given and that they were pressurised to consent despite their hostility in principle to transplantation. Information provided was deemed acceptable by the standards of the time.

6. *The Centre for Reproductive Medicine v Mrs U [2002] Lloyd's Rep Med 259*

   Widow seeking posthumous insemination contested validity of late husband's withdrawal of consent to use of his sperm after death. Allegation of undue influence sustained but deemed not to have overborne the husband's will.

7. *Sidaway v Royal Bethlem and Maudsley Hospital [1985] AC 871*

   Landmark decision by the House of Lords accepting *'Bolam'* principle (*i.e.* professional opinion) as determining how, and how much, information a patient should be given when providing consent to treatment. *'Bolam'* applies to this aspect of the doctor's duty of care as to all others.

8. *Smith v Tunbridge Wells HA [1994] 5 Med LR 334*

   Impotence after repair of rectal prolapse in a young man. Failure to warn of this risk was deemed 'neither reasonable nor responsible', despite some expert opinion to the contrary.

9. *BMA Practical Guide to gaining patient consent.* London: British Medical Association, March 2001

   Set of cards summarising essential information relating to specific areas of consent.

10. *Good Practice in Consent.* HSC 2001/023, Department of Health, November 2001

    Detailed advice from the Department of Health which includes suggested consent forms for specific circumstances. Available at www.doh.gov.uk.

11. *Pearce v United Bristol Healthcare NHS Trust [1998] EWCA Civ 865*

    Judgement in which Lord Woolf promotes the 'reasonable and prudent patient' test '...if there is a significant risk which would affect the judgement of a reasonable patient, then in the normal course it is the responsibility of a doctor to inform the patient of that significant risk'. This formulation of the law was subsequently quoted with approval in the House of Lords in *Chester v Afshar [2004] UKHL 41* and practitioners would be wise to take into account what the reasonable patient would want to know before giving consent, not what the reasonable doctor considers they should be told. In the present case, the risk of allowing pregnancy to continue beyond term was 0.1–0.2%. Although the risk materialised, and the child was stillborn, a risk of this very small magnitude was not considered 'significant' and the court unanimously supported the doctor's decision not to raise it with the mother.

12. *Smith v Barking, Havering & Brentwood HA [1994] 5 Med LR 285*

Unsuccessful action based on alleged failure to give adequate warning. Causation (*i.e.* would consent have been withheld if fully informed) to be considered on a subjective basis, but correct to give weight to objective assessment unless there are extraneous or additional factors. Can claimant discount hindsight and answer reliably after adverse outcome?

13. *McAllister v Lewisham & N Southwark HA and Ors [1994] 5 Med LR 343*

Hemiplegia after operative treatment of a cerebral arteriovenous malformation. Had the claimant been warned, she would have declined surgery or postponed it until she had completed a probationary period of employment.

14. *Re C (Refusal of medical treatment) [1994] 1 All ER 819*; noted in *[1993] 4 Med LR 238*

Schizophrenic patient detained at Broadmoor successfully sought an injunction prohibiting amputation of his gangrenous leg without express, written consent. Criteria for mental competence to refuse life-saving treatment defined by Court of Appeal.

15. *The NHS Trust v Ms T [2004] EWHC 1279 (Fam)*

Patient was brought to hospital hypovolaemic and in respiratory distress following blood loss after self-harming. Her Advance Directive, which refused blood transfusion because she considered her blood 'evil, carrying evil' was declared invalid. She lacked the mental capacity to use and weigh relevant information in arriving at her decision.

16. *Ms B v An NHS Hospital Trust [2002] Lloyd's Rep Med 265*

Vascular abnormality of the high cervical cord resulting in tetraplegia and ventilator dependence. Patient requested that mechanical ventilation be discontinued but her request was not honoured. Court not only deemed the patient competent to refuse treatment but also awarded her nominal damages for trespass to the person. See also revised guidance from the GMC on Withholding and Withdrawing Treatment, July 2002.

17. *Re: AK (Medical Treatment: Consent) [2001] 1 FLR 129*

A 19-year-old suffering from motor neurone disease was able to communicate only by fluttering his eyelids. Through this laborious form of communication, he expressed his wishes to have his ventilator turned off 14 days after he lost the capacity to communicate at all. He was aware that this would inevitably result in his death. The patient was adjudged to be mentally competent, his wishes amounted to a valid advance directive and should be respected. 'The law [in this area] is so completely clear that in a sense a declaration is not really required and the doctors could not have been criticised if they had proceeded with AK's wishes without this application'.

18. *Reference Guide to Consent for examination or treatment*. Department of Health, 2001

    'A patient with capacity is entitled to withdraw consent at any time, including during the performance of a procedure...if stopping the procedure at that point would genuinely put the life of the patient at risk, the practitioner may be entitled to continue until this risk no longer applies' (page 10).

19. *Marshall v Curry [1933] 3DLR 260*

    Canadian case – during a hernia operation, the surgeon discovered a grossly diseased testicle, which he removed as he considered it to be gangrenous and a threat to the patient's life and health. The patient's action in battery was dismissed – the action was reasonable 'in order to save the life or preserve the health of the patient'.

20. Dyer C. *BMJ* 1998; **316**: 955

    Parents of a 10-year-old consented to diagnostic cardiac catheterisation but not balloon dilatation. Doctor acting in perceived best interest of child attempted balloon dilatation with disastrous consequences. Criticised for exceeding his remit and suspended for 6 months by GMC for professional misconduct.

21. *Devi v West Midlands Regional Health Authority [1981] unreported CA*

    Patient consented to uterine repair. Because he believed it was in her best interests, the surgeon carried out sterilisation by occluding fallopian tubes. Liability for battery was admitted.

22. *F v W Berkshire HA [1990] 2 AC 1*

    'Best interests' determine legality of treatment for adult, incompetent patient – in this case, female sterilisation.

23. *Fox v Riverside Health Trust [1995] 6 Med LR 181*

    Feeding is 'treatment' within Section 145 of *Mental Health Act, 1983*; forced feeding is 'treatment' for anorexia nervosa. See also *R v Collins and Ashworth Hospital Authority ex p Brady [2000] Lloyd's Rep Med 359*.

24. *St George's Healthcare NHS Trust v S [1998] 3 All ER 673*

    Compulsory admission under Mental Health Act used wrongly to overrule refusal of consent to caesarean section. Case report makes educational reading – detailing a catalogue of errors in the treatment of this patient.

25. Both parents should consent to religious/non-therapeutic male circumcision. *Re J (A Minor) (Prohibited Steps Order: Circumcision) [2000] 52 BMLR 82*; also sterilisation and immunisation *Re C (A Child) (Immunisation: Parental Rights) (2003) EWCA Civ 1148*

26. Section 3(5) of the *Children Act, 1989* states that where a person has care of a child, but lacks parental responsibility, that person may do 'what is reasonable in all the circumstances of the case for the purpose of safeguarding or promoting the child's welfare'.

27. *Re J (A Minor) (Medical Treatment [1992] 3 Med LR 317*

    A 16-year-old with anorexia nervosa. Parental consent can overrule refusal by a minor, even if over 16 years.

28. *Re E (A Minor) (Wardship: Medical Treatment) [1993] I FLR 386*

    Declaration was granted that blood transfusion would be lawful, notwithstanding objections of parents and child aged 16 years, who shared his parents' Jehovah's Witness faith. The patient, who was ill with leukaemia waited until he was aged 18 years, and then refused further treatment, whereupon his refusal of blood had to be respected and he died.

29. *Gillick v W Norfolk and Wisbech AHA [1986] AC 112*

House of Lords ruling on whether, and in what circumstances, children below 16 years can give valid consent to medical treatment, in this case contraception for a 15-year-old; mother intractably hostile to lack of parental input.

30. *R (Axon) v Secretary of State for Health EWHC 37 (Admin)*

Judicial review re-asserted right of competent minors to receive confidential medical care. See also 'Mother defeated in 'right to know abortion battle', *The Times,* 24 January 2006.

31. *Re R (A Minor) [1992] 3 Med LR 342*

Court of Appeal decision confirming right of parents, guardian or the court to overrule refusal of treatment by a 'Gillick-competent' adolescent: a psychotic girl aged 15 years 10 months. See also *BMJ* 1999; **319**: 209: cardiac transplantation sanctioned in a 15-year-old who refused consent but whose parents had consented. Judge relied upon evidence that child's competence had been eroded by illness.

32. *Glass v UK (ECtHR - Application No 61827/00) – 9.3.2004*

Violent conflict between medical staff and family arose over decision to withhold treatment from disabled 12-year-old. Application for Judicial Review of the Trust's decision failed (*R v Portsmouth Hospital NHS Trust [1999] Lloyd's Rep Med 367*). Court of Appeal held it was inappropriate for Court to declare what a hospital should or should not do as a matter of law. European Court of Human Rights found in favour of parents on ground that in UK law the hospital was obliged to seek approval of the court before administering treatment to which the parents objected. This understanding of the UK law was considered incorrect by the Court of Appeal in *R (on the application of Burke) v GMC & Ors [2005] EWCA Civ 1003*.

33. *Re C (A Minor) (Medical Treatment – Refusal of parental consent) [1997] 8 Med LR 166*

Parents of infant with biliary atresia, both experienced health care workers, refused consent to liver transplant which had been recommended as in child's best interests by three doctors. Strong presumption in favour of preserving life is not an absolute rule and the best interests of child would not be served by overruling the decision of a devoted mother. Compare *Re B (a minor) [1981] 1 WLR 1421*: surgery ordered for duodenal atresia in infant with Down's syndrome.

34. *An NHS Trust v MB [2006] EWHC 507 (Fam)*

Dispute between Trust and parents over proposed withdrawal of treatment from child with spinal muscular atrophy. The court agreed that there should be no escalation of treatment but, contrary to the opinion of medical staff within the hospital and independent experts, declared that ventilation should continue in the child's best interests. 'The views and opinions of both the doctors and the parents must be carefully considered' – but the court will make its own decision.

35. *Wyatt & Wyatt v Portsmouth Hospitals NHS Trust [2005] EWCA Civ 1181*

Court of Appeal review of child's 'best interests' which encompasses medical, social, emotional and all other welfare issues. Upheld declaration that best interests did not require intubation of infant and that pain relief could be administered contrary to parents' objections.

36. *Re F (Mental Patient: Sterilisation) [1990] 2AC 1*

There are some treatments (*e.g.* non-therapeutic sterilisation for incompetent adult patients) which require prior consideration by the court. Generally, however, this is not required when acting in accordance with accepted practice and in the patient's undisputed best interests.

37. *Airedale NHS Trust v Bland [1993] 4 Med LR 39*

Legality of withdrawing treatment from a patient in PVS. Reports from both Court of Appeal and House of Lords.

38. *R-B v Official Solicitor [2000] Lloyd's Rep Med 87*

Vasectomy for Down's syndrome man not in his best interests, although circumstances could change.

39. *Simms v An NHS Trust [2002] EWHC 2734 Fam*

Declaration sought, and granted, that experimental treatment for variant Creutzfeldt-Jakob disease (vCJD) may lawfully be administered to two patients (aged 18 and 16 years) neither of whom was competent to consent on their own behalf. The President of the High Court Family Division considered the treatment, based on a Japanese study in mice, to be in the patients' 'best interests'. Case highlights the permissive effect of a declaration, *i.e.* the court will not order that treatment must be given – notwithstanding the declaration of lawfulness, treatment was not approved by the DH CJD Therapy Advisory Group, the Committee on Safety of Medicines, the Trust's Drug and Therapeutics Committee and the Trust's Clinical Governance and Quality Committee.

40. *R (on the application of Burke) v GMC & Ors [2005] EWCA Civ 1003*

Court of Appeal – judicial review of the GMC guidance on Withholding and Withdrawing Treatment (2002). '...the court does not 'authorise' treatment that would otherwise be unlawful. The court makes a declaration as to whether or not proposed treatment or withdrawal of treatment, will be lawful. Good practice may require medical practitioners to seek such declaration where the legality of proposed treatment is in doubt. This is not, however, something that they are required to do as a matter of law.'

41. The *European Directive on Good Clinical Practice in the Conduct of Clinical Trials 2001/20/EC* was implemented in May 2004 by the *Medicines for Human Use (Clinical Trials) Regulations,* which require that a competent patient 'has given informed consent', 'has been informed of his right to withdraw from the trial' and 'has been given an opportunity to understand the objectives, risks and inconveniences of the trial'.

42. *Law Commission Report: Mental Incapacity. 1995 Law Comm 231*

One of a series of Law Commission Reports on mental incapacity, including comment on research.

43. *Medical Students in Hospitals.* Department of Health HC 91(18)

Obtaining explicit consent to participation of medical students in treatment recommended by DH as 'best practice'. This guidance is subject to review and is likely to be strengthened.

8

Complaints, whistle-blowing and disciplinary proceedings

NHS complaints procedure

Procedures for complaining about services provided by the NHS were revised in 1996 when a uniform complaints system[1] came into effect. Co-incident with the introduction of the new system, the powers of the Health Service Commissioner (Ombudsman) were extended to allow investigation of clinical as well as administrative matters.[2]

The performance of that revised NHS complaints procedure was itself subsequently criticised. In particular, the system was seen to be too slow. On average, NHS Trusts were able to investigate and respond to complaints within the 20-day target in less than 60% of cases.[3] The Ombudsman consistently took longer than a year, on average, to investigate complaints referred to him.[4] There was also criticism of the then second stage of the procedure, which was deemed to be insufficiently independent.[5]

In 2004, the procedure was again revised[6] and 'appeal' to the Healthcare Commission was incorporated as the second stage of the procedure. The procedure now consists of three stages:

Stage I Service providers attempt to resolve complaints by local investigation, followed by a formal written response from the Chief Executive.

Stage II Dissatisfied complainants may ask the Healthcare Commission to review their complaints.

Stage III Referral to the Health Service Commissioner (Ombudsman) is available to complainants who remain dissatisfied with the results of Healthcare Commission involvement.

The NHS complaints system in practice

Parliament has specified that the complaints procedure must cease if a complainant states, in writing, that they intend to take legal action concerning the matters at issue. In practice, however, the complaints procedure may be used to obtain information as a prelude to legal action. Whilst clinicians/trusts may see this as a 'threat', it also affords them the opportunity to investigate the case and set out their position in advance of any legal action and to explain and apologise where appropriate.[7]

Disciplinary proceedings are specifically excluded from the NHS complaints procedure although, if a complaint raises matters of sufficient significance, relevant information can be passed to managerial staff and/or professional regulatory bodies for consideration of further action. Such a punitive step will be unusual and the Court of Appeal has criticised the Health Service Ombudsman for acting beyond her statutory powers and making inappropriate criticisms of medical staff.[8]

Private sector complaints

Independent healthcare providers, operating acute or mental health hospitals or clinics where services are provided by medical practitioners, are required by the *Care Standards Act, 2000 (as amended)* to register with the Healthcare Commission. The *National Minimum Standards and Regulations for Independent Healthcare (2002)* further require the existence of procedures for management of complaints with oversight by the Healthcare Commission.

Whistle-blowing

In its guide *Good Medical Practice*,[9] the General Medical Council (GMC) reminds practitioners of a duty to protect the interests of patients if concerned about the health, conduct or performance of a colleague. It recommends disclosure to the medical or nursing director, chief executive or corresponding post-holders of the employing authority. If local action fails to resolve the problem, practitioners are advised to inform the relevant regulatory body. Concerns that those who complied with this professional duty might be victimised were addressed by the *Public Interest Disclosure Act, 1998* which amended the terms of the *Employment Rights Act, 1996* to: (i)render invalid contractual terms of employment which seek to prohibit disclosure by employees of information in the public interest; and (ii) provide remedies for employees treated detrimentally for making such disclosures.

The type of disclosure protected – information 'in the public interest' – is defined in the statute and requires genuine concern about past, current or likely malpractice, including criminal offences and attempts to conceal wrong-doing. Despite this legislation, many practitioners express disquiet at the possible consequences of discharging the duty to warn of their concerns about the professional competence or behaviour of others.[10]

Professional regulatory proceedings

The GMC is a statutory body, and a registered charity, which regulates the qualification and registration of medical practitioners under the terms of the

Medical Act, 1983, as amended by the *Medical Act, 1983 (Amendment) Order 2002.* The Council is responsible for: (i) promoting high standards in the training and education of doctors; (ii) settings standards of professional competence and conduct; and (iii) registering and licensing doctors to work in the UK whether in the NHS or private practice. Similar provisions exist for the regulation of dental practitioners, nursing staff and other healthcare professionals.

The primary guidance to doctors from the GMC is set out in its publication *Good Medical Practice.* This is currently under review to ensure that the guidance reflects a consensus between public and profession on the standards now expected of doctors (www.gmc-uk.org/guidance/library/ good_medical_practice_review.asp).

In the wake of several high profile medical scandals, subordinate legislation was introduced in 2000 to widen the powers of the GMC, in particular:

➤ Enabling it to impose interim suspension or specific conditions of continuing practice on doctors subject to investigation, if the public interest or the protection of patients so requires.

➤ Requiring that a minimum of 5 years must elapse before those struck off the register can apply for re-admission.

➤ Imposing a statutory duty on the GMC to notify employers or bodies with whom a practitioner contracts to provide services, when fitness-to-practice is under consideration.

Further changes were introduced in 2002, reducing the size of the GMC and increasing the role of lay representation. To counter the criticism that the GMC served the interests of doctors rather than those of patients, the *Medical Act, 1983 (Amendment) Order 2002* stated explicitly that: 'the main objective of the GMC in exercising [its] functions is to protect, promote and maintain the health and safety of the public'.

The GMC's 'fitness-to-practice' procedures were then reformed, as of 1 November 2004, replacing the previous Professional Conduct and Health Committee procedures. Although the investigation of individual cases will be tailored to the nature of the concerns raised, a single fitness-to-practice procedure now applies to matters of alleged misconduct, physical or mental ill-health and alleged deficient performance and there are no longer separate 'streams' for different types of cases.

The GMC's reformed procedures are divided into two separate stages – 'investigation' and 'adjudication'. The detail of the investigation stage will vary depending on the issues in question but may involve obtaining witness statements, seeking evidence from the doctor's employers or other relevant parties or obtaining expert reports on the doctor's health or clinical performance. The purpose of the investigation is to determine if the practitioner's fitness-to-practice is 'impaired' by reason of misconduct, deficient professional performance, criminal conviction or adverse physical or mental health. Following such investigation, two GMC Case Examiners (one lay and one medical) consider the case and decide what action should be taken. This may be:

➤ Case closure with no further action.

➤ Issue of a warning as to future conduct or performance.

➤ Agreement of undertakings with the doctor (*e.g.* to undergo training, treatment or supervision).

➤ Referral to an Interim Orders Panel, for consideration of measures necessary to protect the public pending final determination of the case.

➤ Referral to a Fitness to Practice Panel (FTP Panel), for 'adjudication'.

If the Case Examiners do not agree on the appropriate outcome, the case will be decided by the Investigation Committee.

If a case is referred to a FTP Panel it will hear all the evidence and may then decide to take no action or to issue a warning but it also has the power to:

➤ Put conditions on the doctor's registration (*e.g.* permitting medical work only under supervision or restricted to certain areas of practice) for up to 3 years at a time.

➤ Suspend the doctor's name from the Medical Register for a defined period up to 12 months at a time other than in cases of long-term ill-health in which case suspension may be indefinite.

➤ Erase or remove the doctor's name from the Medical Register so that he will not be able to work as a doctor in Great Britain for at least 5 years.

Difficulty has been experienced in determining just what conduct and circumstances merit professional sanction[11–13] and there may be a tension in some cases between the protection of the public and the reputation of the profession and the rights of practitioners to earn a livelihood. Doctors who consider that a decision has been unfair or otherwise inappropriate are now entitled to appeal to the High Court, whereas prior to 2002 such appeal was to the Privy Council.[14,15] Through such appeals, it has been established that practitioners are entitled, by virtue of the *Human Rights Act, 1998*, to a fair 'trial' by an independent and impartial tribunal, and a number of disciplinary decisions of the GMC have been subject to successful challenge in court either as procedurally flawed or unduly harsh.[16,17] In other cases, decisions taken by the GMC have been upheld.[18,19]

The *NHS Reform and Healthcare Professions Act, 2002*, established the Council for the Regulation of Healthcare Professionals (CHRP) (www.crhp.org.uk). The Council, which has since been renamed as the Council for Healthcare Regulatory Excellence, is empowered to 'appeal' to the High Court decisions taken by healthcare regulators such as those of a FTP Panel of the GMC. It may do so where such appeal is considered desirable for the protection of the public and in relation to any decisions of a FTP Panel that it considers to be unduly lenient either as to fitness to practice or as to penalty, or both. A series of such appeals have been brought by the CRHP, in which the decisions of GMC FTP Panels have been overturned, either as a consequence of procedural irregularity leading to the application of incorrect standards or undue lenience.[20,21] The remit of the CHRP does not extend to review a decision not to refer a complaint to a FTP Panel although conduct once referral has been made may be subject to appeal.[22]

Despite attempts to modernise its procedures and image, the GMC has been subject to criticism as an ineffective regulator and in December 2004, Dame Janet

Smith published her fifth report in the wake of the murders carried out by Dr Harold Shipman (www.the-shipman-inquiry.org.uk/fifthreport.asp). In her report, *Safeguarding Patients: Lessons from the past – Proposals for the Future,* Dame Janet was highly critical of some aspects of medical self-regulation and expressed concerns about whether the GMC's revised 'fitness-to-practice' and revalidation procedures went far enough to secure effective patient protection or safety. The report contains 109 recommendations, which cover:

- the constitution of the GMC and its disciplinary procedures
- handling of complaints, concerns and whistleblowing
- clinical governance, revalidation and appraisal of doctors
- monitoring of general practitioners and the role of primary care trusts (PCTs).

Thereafter, the launch of the GMC's periodic revalidation scheme, which was due to start in April 2005, was postponed. In March 2005, the Chief Medical Officer launched a review of medical revalidation and regulation, including the role and structure of the GMC itself. The outcome of that review is awaited.

Further regulatory control

The National Clinical Assessment Authority, now known as the National Clinical Assessment Service (NCAS) (www.ncaa.nhs.uk), was established in April 2001 to address concerns about the performance of individual practitioners, who may self-refer or be referred by their employer. NCAS can offer recommendations to NHS trusts or employing authorities but responsibility for taking further action rests with the employer. If necessary, NCAS can report individual cases to the GMC.

The Healthcare Commission, (formally known as the Commission for Healthcare Audit and Inspection) is intended to promote quality in healthcare by providing an independent assessment of the standards of service provided by the NHS, private healthcare or voluntary organisations. The Commission's role encompasses duties previously performed by the Commission for Health Improvement (CHI), the NHS value for money work of the Audit Commission, and the independent healthcare work of the National Care Standards Commission (in which respect appeal lies to the Care Standards Tribunal; www.carestandardstribunal.gov.uk).

Action by employing authorities

Health authorities may have grounds to suspend or dismiss doctors in their employ in circumstances of: (i) gross misconduct; (ii) ill health; or (iii) incompetence. In the past, prolonged suspension on full pay during lengthy disciplinary proceedings has resulted in irreversible damage to professional reputations and significant expense to the NHS. Revised procedures,[23,24] agreed between the Department of Health, British Medical Association and British Dental Association, have now been implemented with the intention that cases should be investigated quickly and fairly and, with a focus on patient safety, poorly performing doctors may be retrained and returned to safe practice. The key features are that:

- doctors and dentists employed in the NHS may be disciplined for misconduct under the same locally based procedures that apply to other members of staff;

- issues of ill-health are to be routinely dealt with through the local occupational health service;

- there is a single process for handling capability issues concerning professional competence, with a tight timetable and including early involvement of NCAS. Following advice from NCAS, the matter may be resolved by agreed local action, such as retraining, counselling or performance review. In more serious or difficult cases, final determination on a case is made by a capability panel with external expert medical advice.

In primary care, health authorities (*e.g.* PCTs) are required by the *NHS (Performers Lists) Regulations, 2004* to maintain lists of GPs, including locums and deputies, and only those registered on the list can be employed to perform primary medical services. GPs must also declare to their employing authority any criminal conviction or investigation by another authority and must undertake to co-operate with an assessment by the NCAS if requested to do so by their PCT. Health authorities are permitted to reject, suspend or remove practitioners from local lists on certain grounds (*e.g.* fraud, unsuitability or if inclusion would be prejudicial to efficiency). They are required to do so on other grounds (*e.g.* inadequate knowledge of English or conviction of a criminal offence and sentence to a term of imprisonment in excess of 6 months). The Family Health Services Appeal Authority (FHSAA; www.fhsaa.org.uk) hears appeals against decisions to remove from, or refuse inclusion on, a local list and has powers to disqualify GPs on a national basis and can also do so on application by a health authority. The FHSAA is administered by the NHS Litigation Authority (FHS Appeals Unit; http://www.fhsaa.nhs.uk/fhsaasha/index.html).

It remains to be seen how far this plethora of legislative bodies and procedures will redress the current public perception of medicine as an ill-regulated profession.[25,26] All the evidence suggests that further reform is to be expected. One way or another, the burden of healthcare regulation is unlikely to be reduced.

Suggested further reading

Guidance to support implementation of the *National Health Service (Complaints) Regulations, 2004* on DH website (www.dh.gov.uk) under Policy and Guidance

NHSLA Apologies and Explanations (Circular 02/02) at http://www.nhsla.com/Publications/ under 'Claims Publications'

Bark P. Effective handling of complaints concerning children. *Curr Paediatr* 1997; **7**: 53–56. Of paediatricians, 15% had considered giving up medicine because of the threat or actuality of litigation.

http://www.hse.gov.uk/healthservices/liveissues/concordat.htm. Concordat between bodies inspecting, regulating and auditing healthcare to achieve greater consistency in the inspection of healthcare and to avoid unnecessary overlap

A Guide For Doctors Referred to the GMC, 2005. Guidance booklet on how the GMC deals with referrals about doctors at www.gmc-uk.org (see under 'concerns about doctors')

http://www.gmc-uk.org/about/partners/health_safety_executive.asp – Details of collaborative working between the Health and Safety Executive and General Medical Council with respect to investigation of events or circumstances affecting the welfare of patients or staff

Memorandum of Understanding concerning the investigation of patient safety incidents involving unexpected death or serious untoward harm, February 2006; www.dh.gov.uk – Department of Health, Association of Chief Police Officers and Health & Safety Executive protocol for liaison. 'All experience …shows that a culture in which blame predominates in the handling of errors and adverse incidents creates a climate of fear leading to concealment of safety problems. This can lead potentially to more, rather than fewer, incidents.'

Smith R. The GMC: expediency before principle - further difficult reforms are essential. *BMJ* 2005; **330**: 1–2

References

1. *Complaints – listening, acting, improving*. NHS Executive March 1996.
   Guidance on implementation of the NHS Complaints Procedure (March 1996) circulated to health authorities as EL (96) 19, responding to *Being Heard*, DH 1994: report of Wilson Committee on NHS complaints procedures.

2. The *Health Service Commissioners (Amendment) Act, 1996* repealed the general inhibition on the Ombudsman investigating matters of clinical judgement contained in section 5 of the *Health Service Commissioners Act, 1983*.

3. *Handling Complaints: monitoring the NHS Complaints Procedures (2000-01)* – www.performance.doh.gov.uk/nhscomplaints/main.html

4. *Health Service Ombudsman Annual Reports 2000–01, 2001–02, 2002–03* record average investigation times of 51.4 weeks, 63 weeks and 64 weeks, respectively.

5. *NHS Complaints – making things right*. Department of Health, 2003

6. *Statutory Instrument 2004 No. 1768*. The National Health Service (Complaints) Regulations

7. *NHSLA Apologies and Explanations* – Circular 02/02
   The NHSLA has encouraged the offering of apologies and explanations in appropriate cases. Care should, however, be taken to avoid criticising others and explanations should be factual rather than expressing opinion.

8. *Cavanagh, Blatt & Reymond v The Health Service Commissioner [2005] EWCA Civ 1578*

    A complaint related to the alleged failure of an NHS Trust to provide satisfactory arrangements for treatment of a patient diagnosed with vitamin B_{12} disorder. A wide-ranging investigation was carried out by the Ombudsman, which resulted in criticism of the patient's clinical care and her doctors, against whom there had been no complaint. The Ombudsman's investigation was found to have contravened principles of natural justice, and she had so substantially exceeded her statutory powers that the resulting report was vitiated in its entirety.

9. *Good Medical Practice,* paragraphs 26–28. General Medical Council, 2001

    Duty to protect patients – what practitioners should do if concerned about a colleague.

10. Yamey G. Protecting whistleblowers. *BMJ* 2000; **320**: 70

    Report of a BMA conference on how to protect and empower whistleblowers.

11. *Dad v General Dental Council [2000] Lloyd's Rep Med 299*

    Conviction for a motoring offence did not render practitioner unfit to practise as a dentist. Professional disciplinary proceedings should not impose a second penalty.

12. *Roylance v General Medical Council (on appeal to the Privy Council from the Professional Conduct Committee) [1999] Lloyd's Rep Med 139*

    Unsuccessful appeal by medically qualified Chief Executive of Bristol Royal Infirmary against finding of serious professional misconduct while engaged in administrative duties, and subsequent erasure from the Medical Register.

13. *Rao v GMC [2002] UKPC 21*

    Failure of GP to carry out home visit to patient who then died. Inadequate history taking during telephone consultation admitted. GP appealed, successfully, against restrictive conditions applied to his registration. 'It (the misconduct) was based on a single incident. There was undoubted negligence but something more was required to constitute serious professional misconduct and to attach the stigma of such a finding to a doctor of some 25 years standing with a hitherto unblemished career…for every professional man whose career spans, as this has, many years and many clients there is likely to be at least one case in which for reasons good and bad everything goes wrong.'

14. Dyer C. Privy Council quashes GMC ruling. *BMJ* 2003; **326**: 243

    Appeal by GP who had been removed from Medical Register was upheld by the Privy Council. The doctor had declined to visit a patient at home who had then died. His problems with alcohol, which were unrelated to the charges of misconduct, had been wrongly put to the Professional Conduct Committee (PCC) and could have prejudiced the PCC against him. The GP's registration was re-instated with the condition that his fitness to practice should be considered by the GMC's Health Committee.

15. Dyer O. Privy Council again overturns GMC ruling. *BMJ* 2003; **326**: 415

    Consultant surgeon was re-instated to Medical Register by Privy Council following its finding that the GMC procedures had been procedurally flawed. A series of the surgeon's patients had died from postoperative bleeding. A condition that he should refrain from surgery would have been adequate to protect the public.

16. *Ghosh v General Medical Council [2001] Lloyd's Rep Med 433*

    Professional misconduct proceedings involve a determination of civil rights and obligations and consequently attract protection of Article 6 of European Convention on Human Rights. Privy Council would respect GMC Committee's finding but would not defer to it more than was warranted. Privy Council entitled to consider whether GMC sanction was disproportionate and, if so, substitute another or remit for reconsideration. See also *Carroll v Council for Professions Supplementary To Medicine (Radiographers' Board) [2002] Lloyd's Rep Med 71*. Although this was an unsuccessful appeal against erasure from the register, the report opens with a useful commentary on the implications of the *Human Rights Act, 1998*, the greater willingness of the Privy Council to intervene, the need for penalties to be proportionate to the offence and to be supported by reasons.

17. *Whitfield v GMC [2002] UKPC 62*

    The appellant doctor suffered with alcohol dependency. The GMC Health Committee imposed a complete alcohol ban, and required random breath, blood and urine tests as conditions of continued registration. The Privy Council rejected the appellant's arguments that these conditions interfered with his Article 8 rights to private and family life as scheduled in the Human Rights Act. The appellant had brought his private life into conflict with his public life and his rights could be restricted because of the public interest in protecting his patients.

18. *Gosai v GMC [2003] UKPC 31*

    The appellant doctor was erased from the register for serious professional misconduct after he failed to provide an adequate standard of care to a young patient, and then lied in his evidence to the coroner investigating her death. He applied for restoration on two occasions but failed to show adequate insight into his behaviour. His right to make further applications was suspended indefinitely by the GMC, a decision upheld by the Privy Council.

19. *Gupta v GMC [2001] UKPC 44*

    GP appealed against erasure from register for serious professional misconduct, after permitting her husband, who had previously been struck off the register, to carry out medical procedures in her surgery. The purpose of disciplinary sanctions is to protect the public and the reputation of the profession, not to punish. In this case, however, the appellant's behaviour demonstrated a blatant disregard for the system of registration which is designed to safeguard the interests of patients and to maintain high standards within the profession. Any action other than erasure would be inappropriate.

20. *Council for Regulation of Healthcare Professionals v GMC and Anor [2005] EWHC 579 (Admin)*

    Appeal brought by CRHP against sanction imposed on Professor of Paediatrics arising from conduct associated with expert opinion in child abuse case. Restrictions had been applied to registration, preventing the doctor from engaging in child protection work for 3 years. Appeal allowed – the sanction was unduly lenient in that provision should have been made for the restriction to be reviewed and extended if circumstances or the doctor's conduct required.

21. *Council for Regulation of Healthcare Professionals v GMC and Anor [2006] EWHC 464 (Admin)*

    Procedural irregularity – error in the legal advice given to the Fitness To Practice Panel. Case remitted to the GMC for reconsideration.

22. *R (On the application of the Council for the Regulation of Healthcare Professionals) v GMC and Anor [2005] EWHC 2973(Admin)*

> Allegation that breast examination was inappropriate and without justification resulted in conditions on registration. High Court upheld appeal of CRHP that doctor had been 'undercharged' and that there was sufficient evidence to justify an allegation of indecency. Case remitted to GMC with direction that consideration should be given to a charge of indecent/sexual motivation.

23. *Directions on Disciplinary Proceedings, 2005.*

> Made under the *NHS and Community Care Act 1990*, these Directions require compliance with the procedures set out in Maintaining High Professional Standards in the Modern NHS – available on the Department of Health website (www.dh.gov.uk – at the 'publications and statistics' section). These procedures replace previous arrangements, including the Special Professional Panels - 'the three wise men'.

24. Kmietowicz Z. New suspension procedures aim to cut NHS disciplinary bill. *BMJ* 2005; **330**: 437.

25. Irvine D. The performance of doctors: the new professionalism. *Lancet* 1999; **353**: 1174

> The then GMC President reminds practitioners that professional independence is a privilege requiring competent self-regulation. See also Walshe K. The rise of regulation in the NHS. *BMJ* 2002; **324**: 967.

26. Irvine D. *A Short History of the GMC*. Medical Education 13 February 2006.

> Former President of GMC calls for a GMC directly accountable to Parliament and a change in medical culture to restore the public's trust in the profession.

9

Doctors and the coroner's court

Proceedings in the coroner's court are governed by statute (*The Coroners Act, 1988*, supplemented by *The Coroners Rules, 1984* and the *Coroners (Amendment) Rules, 2005*). Coroners are appointed by a county council, metropolitan or borough council and are identified by the district for which they are responsible. The majority are solicitors but some are medically or dually qualified; a minimum of 5 years' experience is required in either case. Only a minority are full-time coroners.

Apart from a historical role to investigate the finding of treasure trove, the duty of the coroner is to investigate certain deaths. It is not necessary for the death itself to have occurred within the jurisdiction but a coroner is charged with a duty to make enquiry when informed that the body of a person is lying within his jurisdiction and there is reasonable cause to suspect that the death was:

- either violent or unnatural
- or sudden and of unknown cause
- or occurred in prison
- or in such place or circumstances as to require an inquest pursuant to any other Act.

Duty to inform the coroner

Medical practitioners attending a patient in his last illness commonly complete a 'Death Certificate', but this certifies only the medical cause of death. The legal Death Certificate is issued by the Registrar of Births and Deaths.

The Registrar will report the death to the coroner if he is not prepared to issue a formal Death Certificate on the information received. There is no legal obligation on the medical practitioner to report deaths to the coroner but it is courteous to do so if the doctor cannot readily certify the death as being due to natural causes and in the following circumstances:

➤ The cause of death is unknown.

➤ The doctor has not attended the deceased during his last illness.

➤ The doctor neither attended the deceased in the 14 days before death nor saw the body after death.

➤ Death was associated with accident, violence, neglect, illegal abortion or suspicious circumstances.

➤ Death occurred during an operation or before recovery from the effects of an anaesthetic.

➤ Death was caused by industrial disease or poisoning.

Some of these terms are imprecise; however, informal consultation with the coroner will clarify whether or not a death should be reported. A coroner informed of such a death has a discretion to decide that no further investigation is required, with or without a post mortem examination.

The coroner's post mortem examination

The coroner has jurisdiction over the body once a death has been reported to him. He can order a post mortem examination to be undertaken by a practitioner of his choice and does not require the consent of the family or next-of-kin – sometimes family members may be implicated in a death and the coroner's enquiry cannot be frustrated by their refusal to co-operate.

When death occurs in the course of medical treatment, particularly if anxieties have been expressed about the standard of care, the post mortem is usually carried out by an independent pathologist. The pathologist's report is addressed to the coroner and is confidential unless he authorises disclosure. Following receipt of the post mortem examination report, the coroner may conclude that no further investigation is required.

Retention of post mortem tissue

Following the controversy over the retention of post mortem material at Liverpool Children's Hospital and elsewhere, regulation was introduced by the *Coroners Amendment Rules, 2005* and the *Human Tissue Act, 2004*, which makes provision for licensing control of the removal, storage and use of 'relevant material' from deceased persons for specified purposes. Post mortem material of potential relevance to the cause of death can be retained at the discretion of the pathologist acting on behalf of a coroner. The pathologist must then inform the coroner who must specify the maximum period for which the material will be retained. The coroner must inform the family that tissue has been retained and must explain the options for disposal once it is no longer required.

Coroners and the Human Rights Act

The responsibilities of coroners have achieved greater significance by virtue of Article 2 of the European Convention on Human Rights ('everyone's right to life shall be protected by law'). Article 2 imposes on the State the 'substantive obligation' to refrain from taking life without justification and also to establish a framework of measures which will, to the greatest extent reasonably practicable, protect life. Article 2 is also interpreted, by the European Court of Human Rights, as imposing a 'procedural obligation' on the State to investigate deaths occurring in circumstances in which 'agents of the State' are, or may be, in some way implicated.

This procedural obligation is of particular relevance to deaths in custody. It may, however, also apply to deaths of patients detained under the *Mental Health Act, 1983* and deaths in healthcare where there is suspicion of criminality on the part of staff, including gross negligence.[1] In these circumstances, the State is obliged to initiate an effective independent public investigation into the death, involving the deceased's family to an appropriate degree, and normally the inquest alone must satisfy all the rigorous requirements of this 'Article 2 investigation'.[2,3]

The procedural obligation under Article 2 is not, however, engaged in the case of every death whilst under medical care, nor even when death results from 'simple negligence'.[4] The substantive obligation does, however, require that a system should be in place whereby such deaths may be subject to effective investigation. The coroner's inquest forms part, but only part, of this system and the availability of civil and disciplinary proceedings is also relevant in fulfilling the obligations of the State under Article 2.[5] The effect of *The Human Rights Act* on the 'ordinary' inquest may, therefore, be less onerous than may have been feared.

Pre-inquest reviews

The coroners' rules make no provision for pre-inquest reviews, but such meetings are increasingly common in complex cases. They deal with issues such as the witnesses to be called, the scope of the inquest, whether independent expert evidence is needed and whether or not a jury is required. The review also offers a chance for the family to be involved in the process to an appropriate degree and to raise any questions that they hope to have answered.

The inquest

An inquest is an inquiry, not a trial, and there are no parties only 'interested persons'. However, grievances as well as grief are often manifest and, particularly if there are legal representatives, the questioning of witnesses can be quite hostile. The coroner alone decides what evidence, and what witnesses, should be called to assist his investigation and it is up to the coroner to restrict questions to the matters to be explored, namely (i) who the deceased was; and (ii) when, where and how the deceased came by his death.

The coroner is expected to make full, fair and fearless enquiry into the cause of death, but the question 'how' in the normal case is interpreted to mean 'by what means' rather than 'in what broad circumstances'.[6] Where, however, the death occurred in circumstances such that the procedural obligations under Article 2 of the European Convention of Human Rights are engaged (see above), the inquest has a wider ambit and should decide not simply by what means the deceased came by his death but also 'in what circumstances he did so'.[3]

Most inquests are opened and adjourned soon after the death and only evidence of identity is submitted. This represents a public announcement that the coroner has assumed jurisdiction. Unless criminal charges are likely, once the body is formally identified, the coroner may then provide relatives with a certificate allowing burial, cremation or removal of the body outside England.

The inquest is then resumed after relevant witness statements have been obtained. The inquest proceedings are formal but less so than in other courts. The coroner examines on oath or affirmation those witnesses who, in his opinion, can contribute evidence relevant to the questions listed above. The witnesses can then be cross-examined by 'properly interested persons', for example the family of the deceased, or their representatives. Medical practitioners may be called upon to give evidence concerning: (i) the post mortem examination; and (ii) medical aspects of the deceased's terminal illness or underlying state of health.

A witness who fails to attend when summoned may be found guilty of contempt of court[7] and reluctant witnesses may be served with a subpoena. It is also an offence to refuse to answer questions, withhold information, or give evidence known to be erroneous while on oath. That being said, no witness is obliged to answer any question tending to incriminate him, and the coroner is prohibited from framing a verdict in such a way as to appear to determine any question of civil liability, or of criminal liability on the part of a named person. If, during the course of an inquest, it appears to the coroner that a person may be charged with a specific offence such as murder or manslaughter, he must adjourn the hearing and report to the Director of Public Prosecutions.

Inquests into deaths occurring in the course of, or as a result of, medical treatment are a source of particular concern to practitioners. They or their hospital are likely to be represented by a medical defence organisation or hospital solicitor, particularly if grievances are suspected or the family is legally represented. It is recognised that claimants may use the inquest process to obtain information to further a civil claim. Inquests are held in public and may be attended by members of the press. It can therefore prove extremely useful to invite family members to meet with hospital representatives in advance of an inquest, so that if they have questions or matters of concern these may be aired and answered aside from the inhibitions inherent to a public forum.

The coroner's jury

A jury may be called for any inquest but must be called if the death occurred:

1.   While the deceased was in prison, in police custody or resulted from injury caused by a police officer in the execution of his duty.

2.   As a consequence of accident, poisoning or disease, notice of which is required to be given under any Act (*e.g. Health and Safety at Work Act, 1974*).

3.   In circumstances the continuance or possible recurrence of which is prejudicial to the health or safety of the public or any section thereof.

It is this last provision that has received most recent attention in the context of deaths occurring under clinical care where it is alleged that death resulted from systematic failings rather than individual error. Notably, if the coroner is satisfied that steps taken since the relevant events ensure that the same circumstances will not re-occur, then he is not required to summon a jury.[5] There are, therefore, clear benefits for all concerned in ensuring that fatal accidents in clinical care are investigated thoroughly and speedily and that the coroner is informed of any remedial safeguards put in place as a result.

The coroner's verdict

The coroner is not required to return his verdict in any particular form as long as it indicates in concise and ordinary language how the decreased came by his death. However, certain terms are recommended, the most common being:

- death from natural causes

- industrial disease

- dependent or non-dependent abuse of drugs

- accident or misadventure

- suicide

- unlawful killing

- open verdict.

An open verdict is reserved for cases where there is insufficient evidence to reach any of the other conclusions. Increasing use is being made of the descriptive or 'narrative verdict', a neutral statement of the facts leading to death.[8]

Accident or misadventure in the context of deaths related to medical treatment

The term 'misadventure' is commonly misunderstood. Defined as the unintended adverse outcome of an intentional, lawful act, it is well suited to many deaths occurring in the course of treatment. It does not imply negligence, but nor does it refute the possibility of such a finding in a civil court.[9] Many families find the term 'misadventure' more acceptable than mere 'accident' with its connotation that the cause of death was independent of human intervention when it manifestly was not. However, there is no material distinction between the two.

'Lack of care' as a rider to the verdict

The coroner may supplement his verdict by adding the phrase 'and the cause of death was aggravated by lack of care/self-neglect'. This is a phrase where the strict legal definition of 'care' is of paramount importance. It refers to care in the narrow, physical sense and has nothing to do with negligence or breach of duty.[10] The concept is of 'neglect' – gross failure to provide food, liquid, shelter, warmth or basic medical attention for someone in a dependent position who cannot provide it for himself. Neglect (or self-neglect) should not form part of the verdict unless a clear and direct causal connection with the death can be established. Despite these defining criteria, attempts are still made by legal representatives appearing for families of patients dying in contentious circumstances to persuade the coroner to find 'lack of care'. Such applications rarely succeed but may be advanced for financial reasons in the hope that such a finding by the coroner will assist a civil claim. A finding of lack of care requires evidence of absence of care, not that of possibly erroneous care.[11,12]

Recommendations by the coroner

The coroner has the power to refer matters to the appropriate authority or person if by so doing it would enable changes to be made to prevent further similar fatalities.

Challenge to decisions of the coroner

There is no right to appeal the verdict of an inquest. Errors of law or procedural decisions taken by a coroner, including a decision not to hold an inquest,[13,14] may, however, be challenged typically by seeking leave for judicial review in the High Court. In general, the courts are reluctant to order that a new inquest should be held unless it is likely that a different conclusion would be reached or if there has been a failure to comply with the requirements of the Human Rights Act.[5,15,16]

Review and reform of death certification and investigation

In 2001, the Home Office initiated a review of the process of death certification and the content and conduct of inquests. The reviewers reported in June 2003 (www.archive2.official-documents.co.uk/document/cm61/6159/6159.pdf). The murders committed by Dr Harold Shipman also gave rise to an inquiry, which, amongst other matters, considered the role of the coroner in investigations into sudden death. This inquiry produced a report, in July 2003, with recommendations that did not fully accord with those of the Home Office review (www.the-shipman-inquiry.org.uk/thirdreport.asp).

Reform of the coronial system is anticipated and a briefing note issued by the Department of Constitutional Affairs on 6 February 2006 suggests the appointment of a Chief Coroner, legally qualified full-time coroners with medical assistance and greater involvement of bereaved families in the inquest process. A draft Bill is promised as soon as parliamentary time allows.[17]

Suggested further reading

Background information on the role and function of coroners may be accessed on the Department of Constitutional Affairs website at (www.dca.gov.uk/corbur/coron02.htm)

The Human Tissue Act and draft codes of practice may be accessed through the Human Tissue Authority website at www.hta.gov.uk

Lord Chancellor's Department information leaflet for families following sudden death — *When sudden death occurs*, at http://www.dca.gov.uk/corbur/sudden_death.pdf

Home Office briefing for forensic pathologists on the implications of the Human Tissue Act – the restrictions on retention of tissue do not apply to activities, such as determining criminal liability, which are not specified in the Act http://www.homeoffice.gov.uk/documents/human-tissue-act-briefing?

Department of Constitutional Affairs briefing note on Coroners Service Reform http://www.dca.gov.uk/corbur/reform_Coroner_system.pdf

References

1. *R (on the application of Khan) v Secretary of State for Health [2003] EWCA Civ 1129*

   Death of a child associated with maladministration of a potassium infusion during haemodialysis resulting in a blood potassium of 18.9 mmol/l. Allegations of 'medically orchestrated cover-up' resulted as neither the family nor coroner were told of the hyperkalaemia. Following exhumation of the body, at the request of the police, post mortem examination findings were of 'death consistent with potassium poisoning'. The Court of Appeal in this judgement is profoundly critical of the Trust. Although a detailed internal investigation of the case was carried out '...all this activity contained a serious flaw. Nobody had taken any steps at all to tell [the child's] parents what was going on and to involve them in [the investigation]'. Instructive reading for anyone involved in managing the aftermath of untoward clinical incidents.

2. *R (Amin) v Secretary of State for Home Department [2003] UKHL 51*

   The deceased was murdered by his cell mate, a dangerous racist. House of Lords considered the duties of the State in satisfying the procedural obligations of ECHR Article 2. A public inquiry was ordered into the circumstances of the death and the system in prison that allowed the two men to be placed in and remain in joint occupation of the cell.

3. *R (Middleton) v Coroner for West Somersetshire [2004] UKHL 10*

   A murderer committed suicide in prison. Evidence was given that inadequate note had been taken of the prisoner's disturbed state of mind and suicide risk. House of Lords decision that Article 2 imposes a 'procedural obligation to initiate an effective public investigation by an independent official body into any death occurring in circumstances in which it appears that [life has been taken without justification, or there has been a failure to take reasonably practicable steps to protect life] and agents of the State are, or may be, in some way implicated'.

4. *Goodson v HM Coroner for Bedfordshire & Luton [2004] EWHC 2931 Admin*

   Following elective procedure for removal of gallstones, the deceased developed peritonitis and died. Post mortem examination revealed perforation of the duodenum and colon. The High Court found that there is no separate procedural obligation to investigate under Article 2 where a death in hospital raises no more than a potential liability in negligence. In this case, there was at most a possibility of simple negligence which, even if established, would not amount to a breach of Article 2. The coroner was, therefore, not required to conduct his inquest as an investigation for the purpose of Article 2 and the coroner was not required to obtain an independent expert report.

5. *R (Takoushis) v HM Coroner for Inner London & Others [2005] EWCA Civ 14407*

   A voluntary in-patient left psychiatric hospital and was seen preparing to jump off London's Tower Bridge. Having been pulled back from the edge by an American tourist, he was taken to the local A&E Department and assessed as at 'high risk of self-harm'. When left unattended he absconded, to die having jumped into the River Thames. Following insufficient coronial investigation into the systems in place in the hospital to safeguard such patients, the Court of Appeal ordered that a fresh inquest be held. 'Where a person dies as a result of what is arguably medical negligence in an NHS hospital, the State must have a system which provides for the practical and effective investigation of the facts and for the determination of civil liability. Unlike in cases of death in custody, the system does not have to provide for an investigation initiated by the State…' and 'If the coroner is satisfied that because of steps taken since the relevant events, there is no such risk [of continuance or reoccurrence prejudicial to the health and safety of the public], we can see no reason why the coroner should summon a jury…' Sir Anthony Clarke MR (at 64).

6. *R v HM Coroner for Western District of East Sussex ex parte Homberg, Roberts and Manners (1994) 158 JP 357*

   Challenge to conduct of an inquest into deaths caused by arson. The Inquiry must focus on matters directly causative of death. 'How' means by what means, not in what broad circumstances.

7. *Re Dr AS Ryan (1984) 148 JP 569*

   Police surgeon summoned to give evidence at an inquest failed to arrive in time and was ordered to pay a fine. Decision challenged successfully – he had not been properly summoned and could give good explanation for delay.

8. *A(Children), Re [2000] EWCA] Civ 254*

Following lengthy consideration, The Court of Appeal approved surgery to separate the Siamese twins, Jodie and Mary, even though it was inevitable that Mary would thereby die and that it was at least arguable that the separation satisfied the legal criteria for murder. The Manchester Coroner recorded a narrative verdict 'Mary died following surgery separating her from her conjoined twin, which surgery was permitted by an Order of the High Court, confirmed by the Court of Appeal'.

9. *R v HM Coroner for Portsmouth ex parte Anderson [1987] 1 WLR 1640*

Death of a service man from hyperpyrexia on training run; finding of 'accidental death' challenged unsuccessfully. The distinction between 'accident' and 'misadventure' was deemed to be without purpose or effect. See also *R v H M Coroner for Birmingham & Solihull ex parte Cotton (1996) 160 JP 123* – challenge to verdict of natural causes: hospital death from pneumonia in sedated patient with alcoholic liver disease, gastrointestinal bleeding and smoking-related lung damage. Purpose of an inquest is to discover the cause of death, not get a negligence claim on its feet. Questions of medical negligence should be dealt with through the civil courts.

10. *R v H M Coroner for N Humberside ex parte Jamieson [1994] 3 WLR 82*

Court of Appeal Hearing arising from suicide of a prisoner. Extensive review of history and function of coroner's court is followed by a summary of current role and, most importantly, definitive criteria for a finding of 'lack of care'.

11. *R v H M Coroner for Surrey ex parte Wright [1997] 1 All ER 823*

A fit Afro-Caribbean 27-year-old died from cerebral damage after anoxic incident during general anaesthesia for dental extraction. Verdict of accidental death challenged on several grounds including 'If this is not a case of lack of care, what is?' Verdict upheld; no new inquest ordered. Re-emphasis on 'matters of negligence are better decided in a civil action'.

12. *R v H M Coroner for Coventry ex parte O'Reilly (1996) 160 JP 749*

Deceased had fallen at home and, believed to be drunk, was taken into custody. Transferred to hospital 13 hours later, deeply unconscious, where CT showed large intracerebral haematoma. Challenge to verdict of accidental death upheld and new inquest ordered. No reason in principle or logic why accidental death aggravated by lack of care should not be appropriate if circumstances justify, despite obstacle of proving a causal link.

13. *R v HM Coroner for Avon ex parte Smith (1998) 162 JP 403*

Coroner declined to hold an inquest into death of 14-year-old in hospital, admitted with cerebral symptoms. CT, which showed cerebella haemorrhage, not performed for 10 hours despite concern of parents who had earlier lost a son from a 'cerebral episode'. Internal and external enquiries exonerated hospital staff; coroner stated no grounds for inquest because death was 'not unnatural'. Inquest ordered – question of 'natural causes' warranted investigation.

14. *R v HM Coroner for Inner London North ex parte Touche [2001] Lloyd's Rep Med 327*

Maternal death from cerebral haemorrhage occurring after caesarean section for twins. Initially certified as death from natural causes, it subsequently transpired there had been prolonged delay in recognising severe postoperative maternal hypertension. Application to compel the coroner to hold an inquest succeeded at first instance and on appeal: there was evidence to suggest neglect may have contributed to the death, so rendering it 'unnatural'. A combination of unexpectedness and culpable human failing, albeit not sufficient to amount to neglect, will make a death unnatural.

15. *R v HM Coroner for Derbyshire (Scarsdale) ex parte Fletcher (1992) 156 JP 522*

    Deceased had worked as a miner from age 14–50 years. Died aged 65 years from chronic obstructive pulmonary disease and congestive cardiomyopathy. Reported to pneumoconiosis medical panel who concluded pneumoconiosis neither caused nor materially accelerated death. Verdict of natural causes. During investigation to secure compensation, new expert report suggested pneumoconiosis was a contributory factor. Unusually, a new inquest was ordered. Normally mere differences of opinion between experts do not suffice: new evidence not new interpretation is needed.

16. *R v HM Coroner for Birmingham & Solihull ex parte Benton [1997] 8 Med LR 362*

    A 2-year-old with laryngo-tracheo-bronchitis died from bilateral tension pneumothoraces and surgical emphysema soon after emergency bronchoscopy undertaken after prolonged delay in securing hospital admission. Jury permitted only to consider verdict of death from natural causes, which they endorsed by majority of 8:1. Challenge to verdict upheld only in so far as possibility of accident/misadventure should have been left for jury to consider. Finding of 'natural causes' was quashed and a descriptive account was to be given for cause of death. New inquest not ordered.

17. Coroners Service Reform – Briefing Note (February 2006) - see 'Suggested reading'; see also 'Bereaved to gain right to contest death certificates', *The Times* 7 February 2006

10

Doctors and the criminal law

Doctors are not immune from criminality in their private lives. Prosecutions brought against individual practitioners are, however, considered here only in the context of criminal charges arising from actions associated with clinical practice.

Conviction for a criminal offence requires proof beyond reasonable doubt that: (i) the person charged has carried out an unlawful act (*actus reus*); and (ii) in doing so had the necessary guilty state of mind (*mens rea*).

Specific 'elements' for each different offence define the unlawful act and the necessary guilty state of mind. The offence of theft, for example, requires the appropriation of property belonging to another (*actus reus*) with the intention to permanently deprive (*mens rea*). Both must be made out if the prosecution is to succeed. Liability can still be diminished or even avoided if the defendant can advance a valid defence (for example, provocation in the context of murder or 'necessity' in the context of assault).

The standard of proof required in a criminal case – 'beyond reasonable doubt' – is higher than the 'balance of probabilities' which suffices for civil actions.[1] The phrase 'beyond reasonable doubt' does not mean 'beyond a shadow of doubt'. A remote possibility, which is not in the least probable, does not create reasonable doubt. The judge directs the jury on the standard required, often telling them 'they must be satisfied so that they are sure'.

In practice, the legal rules of evidence are observed more stringently in criminal matters. Even so, an accumulation of circumstantial or deduced evidence may suffice to satisfy a jury. There is, however, a presumption of innocence and the burden of proof rests with the prosecution to demonstrate to the satisfaction of the jury that the defendant is guilty.

Assault

The courts are reluctant to find doctors liable for battery with respect to matters arising from consent to medical treatment, unless their actions are wholly indefensible. Remedy relating to consent to medical treatment lies in the civil courts and a claim for damages in negligence. Where, however, consent is obtained by fraud or misrepresentation, criminal liability may arise.[2]

Homicide

Homicide is the unlawful killing of a human being, identified in the context of infants as a life independent from the mother. Murder and manslaughter are both homicide, distinguished by the state of mind of the defendant.

The cause of death must be attributable to the unlawful act, as a matter of fact and of law. Undue vulnerability of the victim (the 'eggshell skull' rule) does not exonerate the perpetrator. Causation in fact is determined by the 'but for' test – but for the act in question, would the victim have died?[3] Causation in law requires exploration of the closeness of the link between the act and the death. Was the act a substantial and operating factor? An example helps to explain this concept – a victim is knocked unconscious and left on the shore where he drowns when the tide comes in. The factual cause of death is drowning: the cause in law on the other hand is the act of the defendant who left his victim on the beach.

The importance of the distinction between causation in fact and in law is apparent when considering the role of medical interventions. Thus two assailants, each convicted of murder, appealed arguing that it was the medical decision to withdraw mechanical ventilation from their victims that caused the deaths.[4] Both appeals failed since at law it was the offences that had led to the deaths.

Similarly, when considering an application for a declaration that withdrawal of mechanical ventilation from a patient with exceptionally severe Guillain-Barré syndrome would not be unlawful,[5] it was accepted that the cause of death would be the disease and not the act of withdrawal, provided the decision to withdraw ventilation had been made in accordance with good medical practice. This decision accords with standard medical thinking – it is the underlying condition which causes the death, not the withdrawal of treatment in a hopeless situation. The context is, however, relevant and, for example, the legal approach would be different if the death of the patient had resulted from withdrawal of treatment by accident or through negligent decision. Thus the propriety of the medical act which intervenes between initiating event or illness and the fatal outcome is to be taken into consideration when considering the legal cause of death, as well as the magnitude of the contribution of each element to the death.

Intention to kill or to cause serious injury is a prerequisite for a conviction of murder. Primary or specific purpose intent exists when a person sets out to secure an objective. Secondary intent (also known as indirect or foresight intent) is a presumption: a man is presumed to intend the consequences of his act if the outcome is a virtual certainty and he is aware, when acting, that this is so. Either primary or secondary intent may satisfy the *mens rea* of murder.

An important distinction must be drawn between intention and motive. Intention refers to what the actor seeks to achieve; motive is the reason or rationale for acting. A benevolent motive does not displace a criminal conviction for murder if the intention to kill is made out at Trial. Thus an intentional killing, even with benign motives, may amount to murder.[6]

Voluntary manslaughter is the likely verdict if a defendant is found guilty of causing death and of having the intention to kill but has successfully pleaded one of a number of defences, usually provocation or diminished responsibility.

The significance lies in the sentence. Murder carries a mandatory life sentence whereas sentencing for manslaughter is at the discretion of the judge.[7,8]

Involuntary manslaughter is a verdict which follows a finding that the defendant caused the death, but without any intention to kill or cause serious injury. It includes death occurring as the result of an unlawful act or, most commonly in the context of medical manslaughter, as a consequence of 'gross negligence' in the discharge of professional responsibilities.

Manslaughter by gross negligence

The definition of gross (*i.e.* criminal) negligence was considered by the Court of Appeal in the course of three appeals, heard simultaneously in 1993, against convictions for manslaughter by an electrician, two junior doctors, and a locum anaesthetist.[9] Two of the appeals succeeded but the third did not. The third appellant, the anaesthetist, appealed, unsuccessfully, to the House of Lords. In the process, the criteria for a finding of involuntary manslaughter by breach of duty were confirmed as:

- the existence of a duty

- breach of the duty causing death

- gross negligence which a jury considers justifies a criminal conviction.

The first two elements of this test are identical to those set out in Chapter 2 as the basis for a civil claim in negligence. The third is the dimension which adds criminality – showing such a high degree of disregard for the safety of others that it amounts to a crime and is deserving of punishment.

The test applies to all professionals who owe a duty of care to those who may reasonably foreseeably come to harm if that duty is not satisfied and gross negligence manslaughter charges have been brought not only against doctors but also, for example, a lorry driver, hydrofoil navigators and an architect.[10]

A jury is entitled to make a finding of gross negligence if evidence is adduced to show that the defendant:

- was indifferent to an obvious risk of injury to health *or*

- had actual foresight of the risk but determined nevertheless to run it *or*

- appreciated the risk and intended to avoid it but displayed such a high degree of negligence in the attempted avoidance as the jury considered justified conviction *or*

- displayed inattention or failure to advert to a serious risk which went beyond 'mere inadvertence' in respect of an obvious and important matter which the defendant's duty demanded he should address.

Given these directions, it is the jury which decides whether the evidence suffices to fulfil one or more of the criteria and, if so, whether the charge of gross negligence has been made out.

Charges of manslaughter by medical negligence have increased in number[11] but the conviction rate is low by comparison with manslaughter cases generally, possibly because of the difficulty of proving, beyond reasonable doubt, that medical error caused the death.[12] The Home Office has proposed a draft bill for the reform of the law on corporate manslaughter. It is intended to make it easier to prosecute companies and other organisations where gross negligence leads to death. The offence is intended to target systematic failings and will apply to NHS bodies, amongst others.[13,14]

Criminal liability for end-of-life decisions – 'mercy killing' and withdrawal of treatment

The conviction of a caring doctor for attempted murder,[6] followed shortly by a House of Lords decision that it would not be unlawful to withdraw artificial nutrition and hydration from a patient in persistent vegetative state,[15] led to the setting up of a House of Lords Committee in 1994[16] to consider the ethical, legal and clinical implications of end-of-life decision-making. The recommendations of the Committee were conservative:

➤ The law should not be changed to permit active euthanasia.

➤ The right of competent patients to refuse medical treatment was strongly endorsed.

➤ The law on suicide[17] should not be changed.

➤ There should be no new offence of 'mercy-killing'.

➤ The mandatory life-sentence for murder should be dropped.

All but the last of the recommendations were accepted by Government. The Committee also acknowledged that it is lawful – indeed proper – to administer drugs to relieve pain notwithstanding an awareness of the probability that they will hasten death, a view confirmed in caselaw both before and after the report was published.[18,19] The essential legal element is the intention of the practitioner – if the primary intention is to relieve suffering, the *mens rea* for a finding of murder is absent. The practitioner may foresee that death is virtually certain after, and perhaps as a consequence of, the treatment, but the presumption that he therefore intends the death is refuted by evidence that his primary intent is to benefit the patient. Some regard this argument as specious, and perhaps in practice it is, but in the absence of a change in the law, this doctrine of 'double effect' enables dying patients to receive pain relief, notwithstanding that it may shorten life.

The courts have considered this issue since the Human Rights Act came into force, and endorsed the stance taken in 1994. Despite repeated unsuccessful attempts to legislate for 'assisted dying', euthanasia and assisted suicide remain unlawful pending action by Parliament to change the law.[20]

Withholding or withdrawing life-sustaining treatment

Termination of life-sustaining treatment may be followed by death in stark, temporal proximity but there is no distinction at law between withholding or withdrawing life support. Both are categorised as an 'omission' (*i.e.* allowing nature to take its course) rather than an action and, in the absence of a duty to treat, an omission to treat does not confer criminal liability.[15] There is, however, a strong presumption that the doctor's duty of care to his patient requires him to take all reasonable steps, in accordance with accepted medical practice, to prolong life. But that presumption is not absolute and a patient's right to self-determination may relieve the doctor of any duty to treat and the refusal of life-saving treatment by a mentally competent adult must be respected.[21] There is also no obligation to commence or continue treatment that is futile (*i.e.* having no realistic prospect of success and being of no benefit to the patient) or that is otherwise not in the patient's best interests (*e.g.* where the burden of treatment is disproportionate to its possible benefits)[22] – see also Chapter 7.

Practical guidance on withholding and withdrawing treatment was issued by the General Medical Council in August 2002[23] and endorsed as lawful by the Court of Appeal in 2005.[24] Withholding or withdrawing medical treatment has been considered by the English courts within the framework of the *Human Rights Act, 1998* but no change of principle emerged.[25,26] It is essential that doctors should not cross the boundary into acting with the intention of ending a patient's life.[24] Withholding or withdrawing treatment is however acceptable, appropriate and lawful provided it is: (i) in accordance with a responsible body of medical opinion; and (ii) in the patient's best interests.[27]

The House of Lords has accepted that nutrition and hydration, when provided by artificial means, constitute 'treatment' – there are risks and benefits and circumstances in which artificial nutrition and hydration (ANH) is clinically contra-indicated.[15] There are, therefore, situations in which ANH is not in the patient's best interests and may lawfully be withheld or discontinued as with other treatments. Given the difficulty of such cases, however, it is recommended that a declaration of lawfulness should be sought from the court in each case in which the withdrawal of ANH is contemplated from a patient in a persistent vegetative state (PVS).[28,29] It is also advisable to take great care before ANH is withdrawn from other physiologically stable patients, particularly if there is any dispute within the healthcare team or between the team and the patient's family.[30] As a first step, obtaining a second opinion or seeking the advice of a clinical ethics committee is a sensible precaution. In difficult cases, the court may be called upon to make an objective assessment of the patient's mental capacity or their best interests[31] but this is not required as a matter of law.[24]

The law as a vehicle for social change

In 1939, an eminent gynaecologist announced that he intended to terminate the pregnancy of a 14-year-old victim of gang rape. He duly did so at a prestigious

London hospital. He was prosecuted and acquitted on a technical interpretation of the relevant statute which permitted abortion in only very restricted circumstances.[32] The case focused attention on the fact that the law on abortion was unsatisfactory and abortion, although unlawful, was widely practised albeit in circumstances which were often unhygienic and dangerous. Subsequent caselaw reflected the preference for properly performed and regulated abortion and was followed ultimately in 1967 by the first Abortion Act.

A number of controversial social and ethical issues have since prompted responsive legislation. Some examples include *The Human Fertilisation and Embryology Act, 1990*, the *Surrogacy Arrangements Act, 1985* and *The Human Tissue Act, 2004*. The law – whether it is defined in the courts or established by legislation – sets the limits of what is deemed to be acceptable practice. The law can and does change in response to social pressures or to new scientific developments. There is no reason why medical practitioners, parliamentarians or judges should be the sole arbiters of ethical dilemmas, but rules need to be set and the law is empowered and indeed required to fulfil that role. It is the duty of all citizens – including medical practitioners – to abide by the law and, if the law assists in defining the boundaries of acceptable medical practice, its intervention is to be welcomed, not feared.

Suggested further reading

Withholding and Withdrawing Life-prolonging Treatments: Good Practice in Decision-making. General Medical Council, August 2002. Sets out guiding principles and describes how they may be applied in specific clinical circumstances

Decisions relating to cardiopulmonary resuscitation, March 2001 – Joint statement of the BMA, RCN and UK Resuscitation Council (www.resus.org.uk)

House of Commons Library research paper into issues underlying assisted dying (January 2000) http://www.parliament.uk/commons/lib/research/rp2000/rp00-008.pdf

Select committee report into Assisted Dying for the Terminally Ill Bill (4 April 2005) http://www.publications.parliament.uk/pa/ld/ldasdy.htm

References

1. 'Raja v Van Hoogstraten'. *The Times* 19 December 2005
   The difference in the standard of proof applied in criminal and civil cases explains why an accused may be acquitted of murder at a criminal trial but held responsible for a man's death at a civil trial.

2. *R v Tabassum [2000] Lloyd's Rep Med 404*
   Consent to breast examination obtained by non-medical 'researcher' was invalid and his actions amounted to indecent assault.

3. 'Doctor, 71, acquitted of murdering three patients'. *The Times* 15 December 2005

   A GP was accused of deliberately terminating the lives of three of his patients, through repeated administration of large doses of morphine and diamorphine. Doctor found not-guilty following evidence that all three patients were close to death before receiving the morphine and their deaths could not be said to have been caused by the drug.

4. *R v Malcherek; R v Steel [1981] 2 All ER 422*

   Discontinuing mechanical ventilation did not suffice to interrupt the chain of causation between initial assault upon two victims and their subsequent death. Appeals against convictions for murder failed.

5. *Auckland Area Health Board v Attorney-General [1993] 4 Med LR 239*

   New Zealand declaration that it would be lawful to withdraw mechanical ventilation from a patient severely affected by Guillain Barré syndrome. Question explored was whether death was caused by the disease (yes) or the withdrawal of ventilation.

6. *R v Cox (1992) 12 BMLR 38* (and see legal commentary *BMJ* 1992; **305**: 731)

   Consultant rheumatologist administered intravenous potassium chloride to a woman terminally ill from chronic rheumatoid arthritis, in 'uncontrollable' pain, who begged to die and whose family supported her decision. Conviction for attempted murder (cause of death unproven because body had been cremated before charges were brought).

7. 'Mother who killed Down's son spared jail'. *The Times* 3 November 2005

   Mother admitted killing her son, and was convicted of manslaughter by reason of diminished responsibility.

8. 'Husband who killed his 'soul mate' goes free'. *Daily Telegraph* 3 September 2005

   Defendant suffocated his terminally-ill wife at her request, that request having been overheard by a visiting doctor. Charge of murder dropped after plea of guilty to manslaughter on grounds of diminished responsibility. Sentence – 3 year conditional discharge.

9. *R v Holloway; R v Adomako; R v Prentice & Sullman [1993] 4 Med LR 304*

   This report does not include the facts of *R v Holloway* – an electrician whose faulty wiring of a central heating system caused death by electrocution – but the Court of Appeal set out principles applying to all three cases. The anaesthetic death involved failure to recognise disconnection of the ventilator; the third case arose from a fatal injection of vincristine into the theca in a patient receiving regular intrathecal methotrexate and intravenous vincristine. The appeals of Holloway, Prentice and Sullman were allowed, their convictions being quashed. Adomako's appeal failed, as did his appeal to the House of Lords (*R v Adomako [1994] 5 Med LR 277*).

10. 'Architect accused of legionnaires' deaths'. *The Guardian* 9 February 2005

    Prosecution of a local authority employee for alleged failure to maintain an air-conditioning system, to an extent that was grossly negligent. The jury failed to reach a verdict on the manslaughter charges, but found the defendant guilty of breaching health and safety laws.

11. Ferner R. Medication errors that have led to manslaughter charges. *BMJ* 2000; **321**: 1212–1216

    Review confined to medication errors. Incidence of charges of medical manslaughter have increased from about one case every 4 years (1972–1990) to almost two each year (1990–2000). This reflects a policy decision by the Crown Prosecution Service to prosecute cases of suspected gross negligence or recklessness in the workplace. See also *BMJ* 2002; **325**: 63 for summary of more recent cases.

12. Dyer C. Surgeons cleared of manslaughter after removing wrong kidney. *BMJ* 2002; **325**: 6

Delayed death from multiple organ failure after removal of sole functioning kidney in an elderly man. Trial for manslaughter collapsed because pathologist 'could not be sure' the nephrectomy had caused the death.

13. *Proposals for reform of the law relating to corporate manslaughter* at www.homeoffice.gov.uk/documents/2005-corporate-manslaughter

Includes the government response (8 March 2006) to the Home Affairs and Work and Pensions Committees' considerations of the draft Bill.

14. 'Rethink on corporate killing'. *The Times* 17 January 2006

Michael Caplan QC comments on the draft corporate manslaughter legislation.

15. *Airedale NHS Trust v Bland [1993] 4 Med LR 39*

Hugely significant decision of the House of Lords that withdrawal of artificial nutrition and hydration (ANH) from a patient in persistent vegetative state would not be unlawful. The decision was premised on a recognition that ANH constituted medical treatment, that there was no legal distinction between withholding and withdrawing treatment, and that there were circumstances in which withdrawal of treatment was in the patient's best interests.

16. *Select Committee on Medical Ethics, House of Lords Report*. HMSO 1994

Legal and ethical analysis of end-of-life decisions. Law should not be changed to permit active euthanasia. Offence of 'mercy-killing' not recommended; suggestion to drop mandatory life sentence for murder rejected by Government.

17. *Suicide Act, 1961*

Suicide is no longer a criminal offence. It remains, however, an offence to assist a suicide. 'Son questioned over assisted suicide'. *The Telegraph* 7 May 2006 - after accompanying his mother to the Swiss Dignitas Centre, where she committed suicide.

18. *R v Bodkin Adams [1957] Crim LR 365*

GP acquitted of murder by administration of increasing doses of opiates to elderly patients. A doctor 'is entitled to do all that is proper and necessary to relieve pain and suffering, even if the measures he takes may incidentally shorten life' per J Devlin. See also *R v Arthur (1981) 12 BMLR 1*; acquittal of consultant paediatrician charged with attempted murder by prescribing 'dihydrocodeine and nursing care only' for a neonate with Down's syndrome rejected by her mother.

19. Dyer C. *BMJ* 1999; **318**:1306

Unwise public declaration by a GP that he had helped a number of patients to have pain-free deaths led to prosecution for murder. Unanimous verdict of 'not guilty'. GP's considerate treatment was applauded by the judge. See Gillon R, Doyal L. *BMJ* 1999; **318**: 1431 for discussion of ethical doctrine of 'double effect'.

20. *R v Director of Public Prosecutions ex parte Pretty and Secretary of State for the Home Department [2001] 63 BMLR 1*

Patient with terminal motor neurone disease sought an assurance that no criminal charge would be brought against her husband if he assisted her to die when she considered life intolerable. Framed in terms of the *Human Rights Act, 1998*, the application failed at first instance and on appeal to the Divisional Court, House of Lords and European Court (European Court Reference 2346/02; 29.04.02).

21. *Ms B v An NHS Hospital Trust [2002] Lloyd's Rep Med 265*

Vascular abnormality of the high cervical cord resulting in tetraplegia and ventilator dependence. Patient requested that mechanical ventilation be discontinued. Court not only deemed the patient competent to withhold consent but also awarded damages for trespass to the person.

22. *South Buckinghamshire NHS Trust v R (A Patient) [1996] 7 Med LR 401*

A 23-year-old existed in a 'low awareness state'. No obligation to treat if, in all the circumstances, life would be so afflicted as to be intolerable. See also *Airedale NHS Trust v Bland [1993] 4 Med LR 39*[15] above where treatment withdrawal was justified on grounds of futility.

23. *Withholding and Withdrawing Life-prolonging Treatments: Good Practice in Decision-making.* General Medical Council, August 2002

Sets out guiding principles and describes their application in specific clinical circumstances. Endorsed as lawful in judicial review proceedings (see *R(Burke) v GMC [2005] EWCA Civ* 1003[24]).

24. *R(Burke) v GMC [2005] EWCA Civ 1003*

Judicial review of the GMC guidance on withholding and withdrawing treatment,[23] which the Court of Appeal considered to be lawful. 'For a doctor deliberately to interrupt life-prolonging treatment in the face of a competent adult patient's expressed wish to be kept alive, with the intention of thereby terminating the patient's life, would leave the doctor with no answer to a charge of murder'; '…the court does not 'authorise' treatment that would otherwise be unlawful. The court makes a declaration as to whether or not proposed treatment or withdrawal of treatment, will be lawful. Good practice may require medical practitioners to seek such declaration where the legality of proposed treatment is in doubt. This is not, however, something that they are required to do as a matter of law'. Ld Phillips of Worth MR

25 *A National Health Service Trust v D and Ors [2000] Lloyd's Rep Med 411*

Successful application by NHS Trust for a declaration that a 19-month-old child with irreversible lung disease be treated in accordance with his best interests as judged by paediatrician responsible for his care, including non-resuscitation from cardiac or respiratory arrest. No infringement of right to life (European Convention on Human Rights, Article 2); right under Article 3 (no inhuman and degrading treatment) protected.

26 *NHS Trust A v Mrs M; NHS Trust v Mrs H [2001] Lloyd's Med Law Rep 28*

Withdrawal of hydration and nutrition from patients in PVS was deemed by the President of the Family Division of the High Court not to contravene relevant Articles of the European Convention on Human Rights.

27. *Re J (A Minor) [1993] 4 Med LR 21*

Infant with profound neurological disability and frequent convulsions compromising respiration. Court of Appeal reversed a decision requiring that child be given life-prolonging treatment, including mechanical ventilation. There is no obligation to provide treatment which, in *bona fide* opinion of practitioner, is not in patient's best interests. It would be 'wholly inconsistent with the law' to order treatment contrary to doctor's clinical judgement.

28. Wade DT, Johnston C. The permanent vegetative state. *BMJ* 1999; **319**: 841
Review of clinical features plus practical guide on steps required to obtain court's approval to discontinue treatment.

29. Practice Note (Official Solicitor: Declaratory Proceedings - medical and welfare decisions for adults who lack capacity) www.officialsolicitor.gov.uk/

30. Bliss MR. Is an apology called for? *BMJ* 2000: **320**: 67
Critical analysis by a consultant geriatrician of the reprimand and suspension of a GP for ordering withdrawal of nutritional supplements from a demented elderly patient. Reported to police by nurses; police referred to GMC.

31. *NHS Trust v A & Anor [2005] EWCA Civ 1145*
An 86-year-old patient, in chronic renal failure, with severe cardiac disease required respiratory support. Court of Appeal upheld declarations that withdrawal of life-sustaining treatment would be lawful notwithstanding objections of family on religious grounds. Further invasive treatment would not be in patient's best interests.

32. *R v Bourne [1939] 1 KB 687*
Criminal prosecution for procuring a miscarriage in contravention of *Offences Against the Person Act, 1861*. Not unlawful if done in good faith for sole purpose of preserving the life of the mother – interpreted to include adverse consequences to physical health short of death.

11

Glossary of legal terms, phrases and abbreviations

Act of parliament	Completed parliamentary legislation
Actus reus	Factual element of a criminal offence
ADR	Alternative Dispute Resolution – alternatives to litigation
Aggravated damages	Additional compensation for injurious personal conduct
Appellate Courts	Courts hearing appeals from decisions of a lower court or judicial officer
Assault	Threat causing apprehension of immediate physical contact
Battery	Non-consensual touching
Burden of proof	Party on whom onus lies to prove its case
CFA	Conditional Fee Agreement
CNST	Clinical Negligence Scheme for Trusts
Common law	Body of decided English legal cases (*i.e.* 'caselaw')
Competence	Sufficiency of mental faculties to take legally valid decisions
Consideration	The price of a contractual agreement
Contract	A legally enforceable agreement
Damages	Financial compensation
Inquest	Proceedings and conclusion of coroner's court
Issue of proceedings	First formal step in civil litigation
Judicial Review	Remedy for wrongful exercise of administrative power
Legal aid	State-funded financial assistance for legal proceedings
Limitation	Extinguishing of legal right of action by passage of time
Litigation Friend	Court-approved legal representative
LSC	Legal Services Commission
MDOs	Medical defence organisations

Mens rea	A criminally culpable state of mind
Misadventure	A sub-section of accident in Coroner's verdicts
Misfeasance	Wrong-doing
Multiplicand	Net annual value of an ongoing loss
Multiplier	Variable reflecting period of a loss, discounted for early receipt
NCAA	National Clinical Assessment Authority
Neglect	Gross failure to provide basic necessities
Negligence	Culpable transgression of a duty
NHSLA	National Health Service Litigation Authority
NPSA	National Patient Safety Agency
PCT	Primary Care Trust
Parliamentary Bill	A proposed item of parliamentary legislation
Particulars of Claim	Formal statement of claimant's case
Pleadings	Collection of formal documents encapsulating an action: the term Statement of Case is now preferred
Precedent	A binding judicial decision
Privy Council	Body of advisers to the Sovereign, appointed on the advice of Ministers: until 2002, the Judicial Committee of Privy Council heard appeals from professional disciplinary bodies (*e.g.* GMC)
Proceedings	Formal legal action
Quantum	The financial value of a claim for compensation
Res ipsa loquitur	Aphorism meaning 'the thing speaks for itself'
Service (of documents)	Delivery by a legally accepted method
SHA	Strategic Health Authority
Standard of proof	Degree of certainty to be achieved for an action to succeed
Statement of case	Term introduced by Civil Procedure Rules 1999 to replace Pleadings
Statute	An Act of Parliament
Statutory Instrument	Subordinate (delegated) legislation permitted by a parent Act
Tort	Civil wrong-doing not including breach of contract
Vicarious liability	Liability for injury caused by another (*e.g.* an employee)

12

Index